A Pocket Guide to *Plants & Gardening*

A Pocket Guide to Plants & Gardening

Elizabeth McCorquodale

black dog publishing
london uk

Contents

Garden Wildlife

The History of Gardening

The Life of Plants

What is a Plant?

It would seem easy enough to define exactly what makes a plant a plant, but scientists have been wrangling over this issue for years. A relatively neat and tidy definition is to include all green plants, all the green algae that is able to photosynthesise, as well as mosses, liverworts, hornworts and stoneworts. This group as a whole goes under the name of *Viridiplantae* (green plants) or simply *Plantae*.

However there are exceptions to even this tidy definition. There are some true plants that have lost the ability to photosynthesise. Parasites, like the dodder plant, rely on other plants to do the hard work for them, stealing food directly from the "veins", the vascular system, of other green plants; these *are* included. There is also a particular group of cyanobacteria and other plant-like bacteria that are able to photosynthesise, but although they contain chloroplasts they are *not* classified as plants nor are fungi or any of the lichens, even though some of them look remarkably like mosses.

Classifying an organism as belonging to one kingdom or another is all about heritage and as science is conducted more and more on a genetic level, tracing the trail of an organism's ancient ancestry becomes increasingly complicated.

Without plants there would be no us.

Vascular Plants

Vascular plants are plants that have a system of vein-like tubes for moving water and nutrients around their leaves, stem and roots. Non-vascular plants have no such system and, like mosses and liverworts, have developed different ways of transporting food and water around.

All the organisms in *Viridiplantae* contain chlorophyll a and b—there are several types of chlorophyll—and are able to store starch for energy—as in, for example, a parsnip root—and have cellulose in their rigid cell walls—the stuff that is used to make cellophane wrapping—and they have plastids—small organs such as chloroplasts—contained within their cells that are bound by only two membranes.

The Chaotic Kingdom of Life

2,300 years ago the Greek philosopher Aristotle divided the living world into two Kingdoms: *Animalia*, organisms that were able to move around in search of food and a mate and *Plantae*, those that were unable to move. At this time, before microscopic investigation—even before the invention of spectacles—these two groups were all that were needed and for the following 1,800 years nothing really changed. The world of plants and animals, it was thought, were perfectly described by a handful of classical Greek scholars and there was no need to do any more. Any natural curiosity (and there is little evidence that there was much curiosity) was swiftly quashed by the religious leaders of the time. It wasn't until the fifteenth century that this pervasive and puzzling disinclination to observe the natural world as it really was, slowly—very slowly—began to be challenged and it wasn't until plants began to be seen as things other than the source of food, medicine and magic that the scholars of the time glanced up from their herbals and began to look at the natural world in a whole new light. The Dark Ages moved forward into the Age of Enlightenment.

This age of discovery revealed a world richer in living organisms than had previously been imagined. Strange plants began to pour in from the New World and from the Far East. With the invention of the microscope in the late sixteenth century and the subsequent discovery of microscopic life, the easy delineation between plants and animals became blurred—Swedish botanist Linnaeus added another Kingdom when he did his great work on classification in the first half of the eighteenth century—and slowly the number of Kingdoms crept up from the original two to their current numbers.

In 1969 fungi, algae and bacteria were unceremoniously hoiked out of Plantae and given their own Kingdom. Further discoveries dictated that there needed to be a level above Kingdom and the Domain was introduced. Currently, and depending on which school of thought you choose to follow, there are Domains (two), Super Kingdoms (two or three depending on which system you follow), Kingdoms (five in most of the world, six in America), Phylum, Class, Order, Genus and Species. In between some on these there are subcategories. The family tree is tall and many branched.

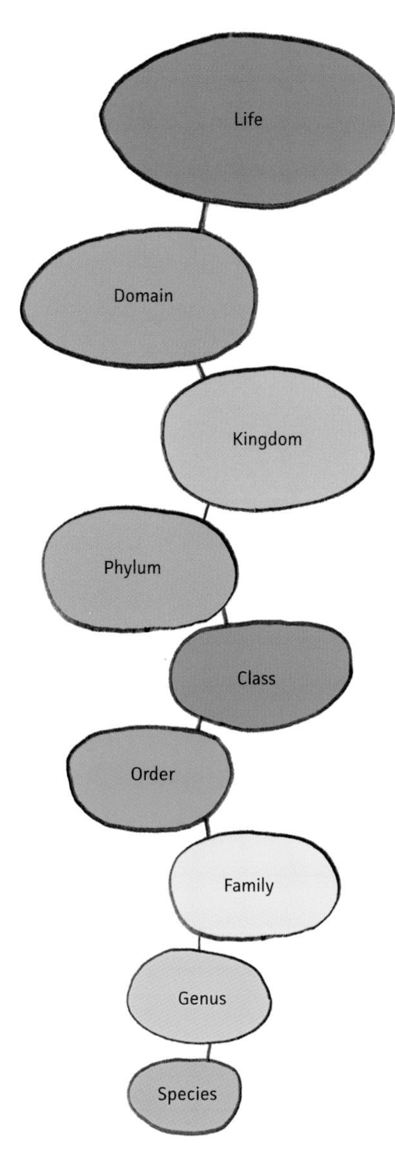

Angiosperms and Gymnosperms

Angiosperms, gymnosperms, mosses, ferns, plant algae and selaginella are the major groupings within the Plantae family and are classified according to their structure and how they reproduce. Plants with flowers are called angiosperms, and those without are called gymnosperms. Angiosperms are a highly successful group of plants containing about 250,000 to 300,000 species of flowering plants worldwide. In contrast gymnosperms, the non-flowering group which contain conifers, cycads, the single genus Ginkgo and an odd little group called gnetophytes, only amount to a paltry 947 species in the world.

Algae, Fungi, Lichen... plants or not?

Fungi and many types of algae are not classed as plants. In fact fungi have more in common—genetically speaking—with the animal kingdom than with the plant kingdom.

Algae is just a general term for many unrelated organisms, and has no true scientific definition. Giant seaweeds—the kind you swim through at the seaside—are classed as algae, as are the transparent microscopic diatoms that swim about with the aid of tiny hairs. Some algae are classed as plants and some as bacteria. Some create such a close partnership with fungi that for all intents and purposes, they do not exist as separate organisms.

Lichens are a combination of fungi and algae... the fungi provide the minerals and the algae carries out the photosynthesis to provide the carbohydrates in the form of sugars.

Flowers

The sole purpose of flowers is reproduction. Flowers, tiny or extravagant, are designed to assist fertilisation by attracting pollinating animals. They come in all shapes and sizes, from the giant stinking corpse flower *Rafflessia*, at almost a metre across, to the tiny *Wolffia*, a type of duckweed, at 1/1000th of that, less than one millimetre across.

Colourful petals, often with markings visible under ultraviolet light, act as signals and landing pads to insects and other pollinators. Those that are designed to be pollinated by moths and bats are often white and highly scented. Flat and open flowers are attractive to bees, while short funnels attract butterflies.

Some plants have evolved to fool their pollinators in some way; some even go to the bother of only pretending to offer nectar by presenting a glistening, nectarless orb as a lure. Many mimic the colour or shape of other plants that offer rich nectar rewards, but these cheats fail to give even a sip of the sugary stuff.

Scientists and gardeners took a long time to figure out the story behind nectar and nectaries. Some people thought nectar trapped pollen, others that it was a waste product that bees kindly removed and others that it was there to feed the developing ovules. Konrad Sprengel, a rather eccentric eighteenth century priest who lost his parish and his income because he routinely forgot to deliver his Sunday sermons to his parishioners, was the gentleman who established that nectar is a lure for pollinators.

Plants without showy flowers are almost always wind pollinated. Their flowers are simple and open, usually lacking petals so there is less to interrupt the flow of the wind; Catkins of birch and alder and the upright flowering stem of grasses are typical examples of wind pollinated flowers.

Water also plays a part, with roughly two per cent of plants worldwide pollinated in this way. While most aquatic plants still use animals for pollination there are a significant number who use water currents to distribute their pollen—pond weed is a common example. Unsurprisingly the miniscule *Wolffia* is water pollinated.

Bee orchids mimic female bees in both appearance and scent, emitting sex pheramones to lure them in. Orchids are unsurpassed in the field of sexual mimicry and it is thought that up to 60 per cent of orchids are pollinated in this way.

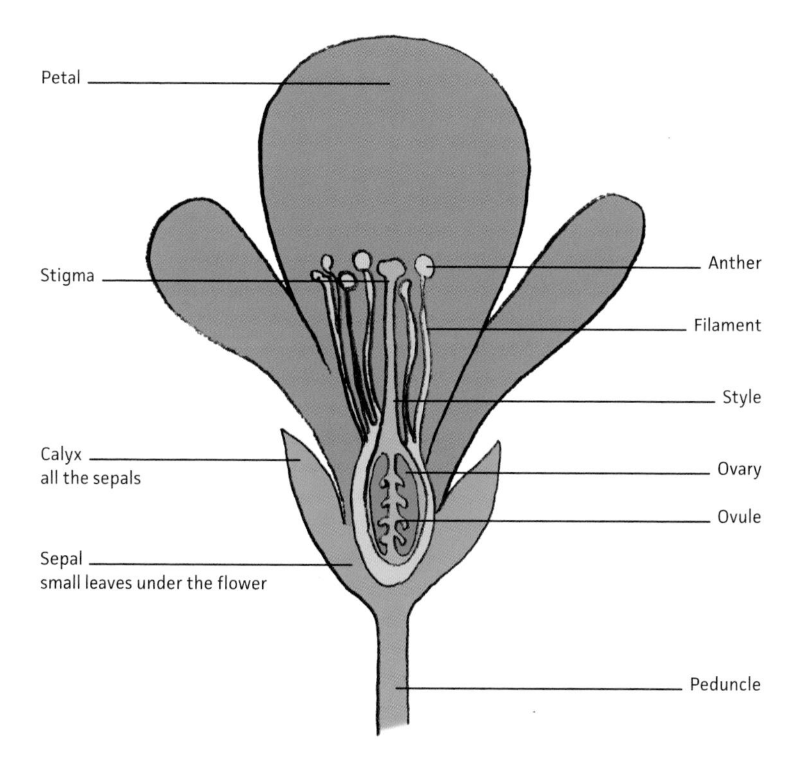
Petal
Stigma
Calyx
all the sepals
Sepal
small leaves under the flower
Anther
Filament
Style
Ovary
Ovule
Peduncle

Pollination

The basic anatomy of pollination is that the male part of the flower is called the stamen and it is made up of the filament and the anther. The anther contains the pollen, which contains the sperm. The female part of the flower is called the pistil and it is made up of the stigma, the style, and the ovary. The ovary contains the egg cell called the ovule.

Pollination occurs when a grain of pollen is released from the anther and arrives on the stigma. Sugars on the stigma either stimulate the pollen to germinate if it is compatible, or inhibit growth if the stigma is incompatible, perhaps because it is from a different species, or from a plant that is designed only for cross-pollination. The pollen grain itself does not travel down the style to the waiting egg cell; because the sperm cells themselves are immobile, the pollen grain germinates and sends out a tube, carrying two sperm cells in the tip. This tube is *chemo*trophic; it grows towards a source of chemicals. The source of the chemicals is the ovule.

Once the tip of the pollen tube reaches its goal a magical thing happens. As it touches the ovary the tip of the tube explodes and ejects the two sperm cells. One sperm fuses with the egg cell within the ovary to form the new plant embryo (you can see the embryo plainly if you split a runner bean seed before it germinates). The other sperm fuses with *both* the nuclei in the central cell inside the ovary to make the endosperm, the food source for the growing plant. This endosperm is rich in oils, starch and protein. At first it is liquid, solidifying as it matures. The best known example of liquid endosperm is coconut milk, which later turns into the white flesh of the coconut. Other familiar examples of endosperm are rice, wheat, oats and barley, the very parts of these grasses that are ground into flour. The wheat germ that is touted as super nutritious is the embryo and the super-fibre food, bran, is the seed coat.

There are other methods of pollination. Cycads, those leathery-leaved cone-bearing palms from the tropics and sub-tropics, often employ a particular beetle to carry the pollen from male to female. The pollen, with the aid of a tail called a flagella then swims towards the egg and fertilisation occurs.

Conifers and ginkgo are wind pollinated. Having been released in clouds and by chance landed on the target of an exposed flowerless ovule (usually handily arranged at the tip of a stem or branch to maximise the chance of pollination) the pollen enters the ovule via a minute opening. From there the pollen grain germinates a pollen tube which searches out the egg cell. Wind pollination is a haphazard affair, requiring the male to release vast numbers of pollen grains in the hope that some will be blown in the right direction and land on a receptive ovule. It is because of this practice that you may suffer from hay fever in the spring.

The ovule becomes the seed and the ovary becomes the fruit.

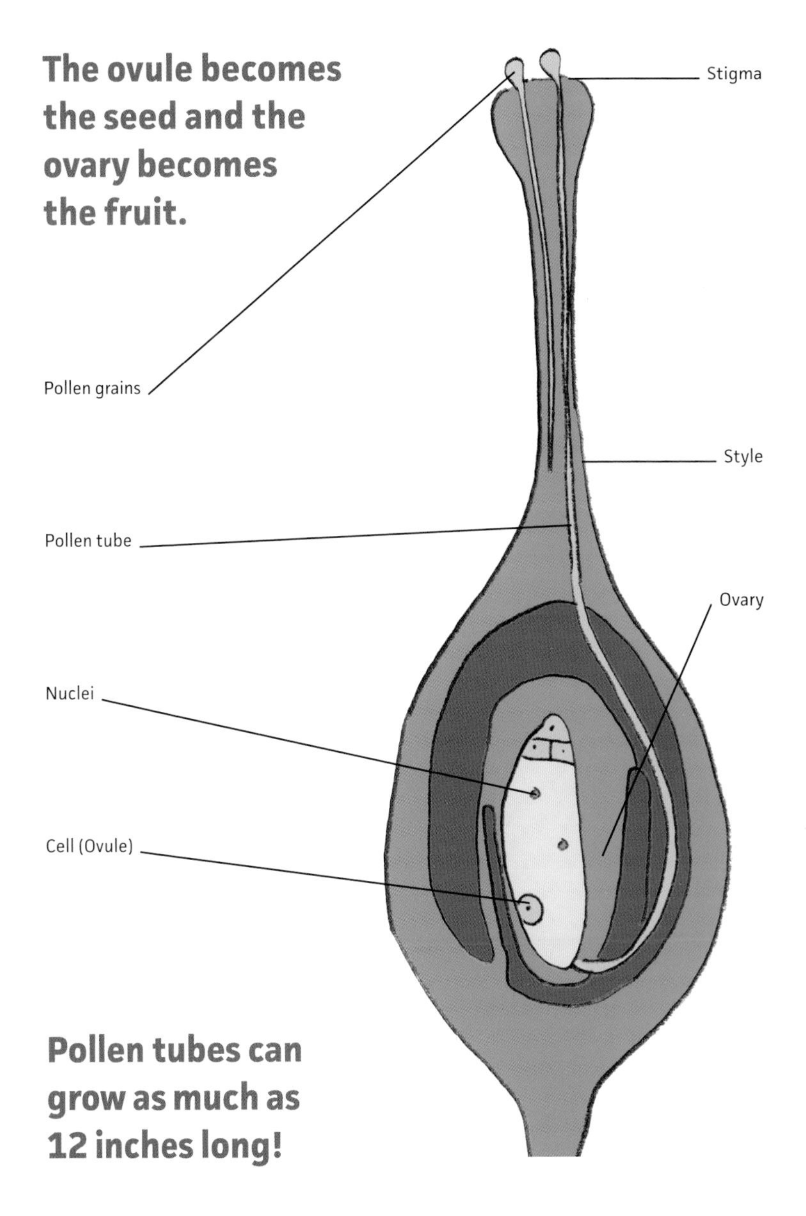

Pollen tubes can grow as much as 12 inches long!

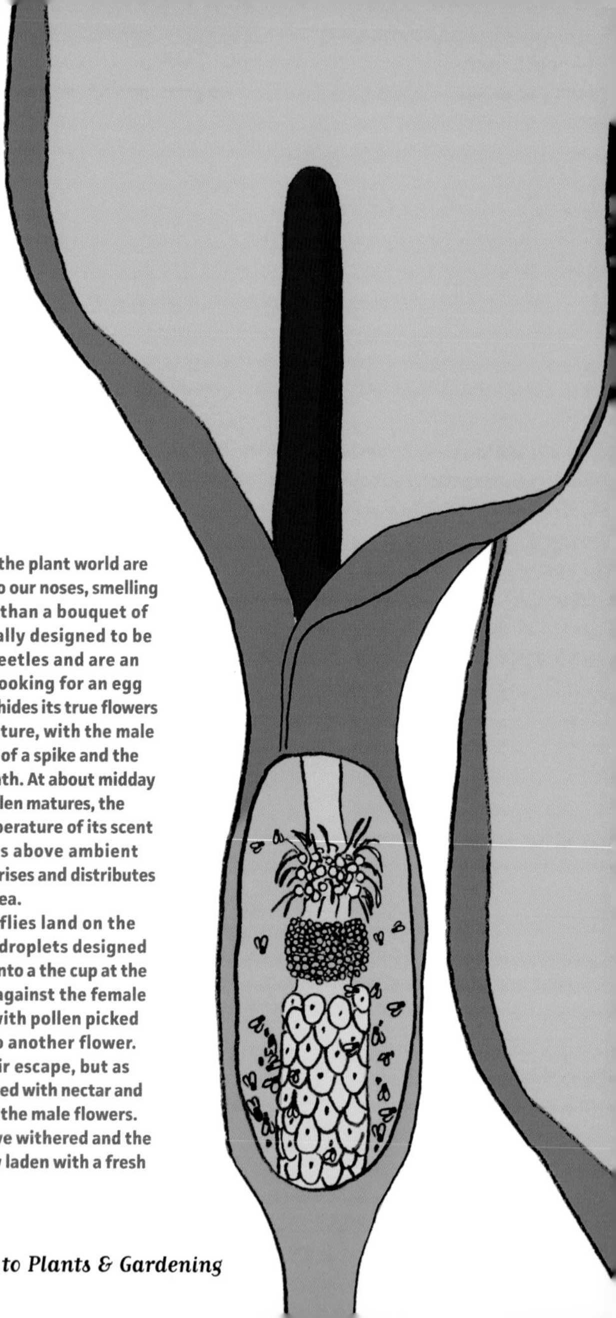

Some of the scents in the plant world are less than appealing to our noses, smelling more like rotting flesh than a bouquet of roses! These are generally designed to be pollinated by flies or beetles and are an enticement to insects looking for an egg laying site. The arum lily hides its true flowers deep in the flower structure, with the male flowers arranged on top of a spike and the female flowers underneath. At about midday on the day before the pollen matures, the plant increases the temperature of its scent structure to 15 degrees above ambient temperature which vaporises and distributes the odour over a wide area.

Drawn to the scent, flies land on the sheath, slip on the oily droplets designed for the purpose and fall into a the cup at the base. There they brush against the female flowers, dusting them with pollen picked up on a previous visit to another flower. Spiky hairs prevent their escape, but as they rest they are rewarded with nectar and dusted with pollen from the male flowers. By morning the hairs have withered and the fly is able to escape, now laden with a fresh load of pollen.

Some plants practice a wonderful trick to release their pollen called rapid plant movement. *Morus alba*, the white mulberry, is remarkable for its incredibly rapid pollen release. The stamens behave as catapults, releasing stored elastic energy and hurling the pollen into the air at over half the speed of sound.

The majority of plants are monoicious (separate male and female flowers on the same plant) or hermaphrodite (bearing flowers that each have both male and female parts) but that isn't to say that they are self-contained in the pollination department. Most, indeed, are self-sterile, having some mechanism in place that prevents flowers from fertilising other flowers on the same plant.

On some plants the pollen and the ovules ripen at different times, on others the arrangement of the style high up above the pollen-bearing stamens makes it all but impossible for accidental self-fertilisation.

Some flowers operate a death-squad attitude towards pollen from their own plant which means that as soon as the unfortunate pollen grain lands on the stigma of a flower from the same plant, a chemical on the sticky stigma pad murders it! Only pollen from other plants is accepted, ensuring genetic diversity by cross-pollination.

Seeds & Seed Dispersal

If you thought the whole point of a seed was to grow into a new plant as soon as conditions allow, this next bit may take some getting used to. A seed is indeed designed to protect the embryo inside until conditions are suitable for growth, but it is also designed to distribute individual plants *and* to maintain a reserve of potential plants to ensure the continuation of the population.

If all the seeds from a single plant were to drop at the feet of the parent and germinate at the same time it would soon be a rather crowded neighbourhood. Nutrients, water and light would be in short supply and the community would collapse. Evolution, the great system of trial and error, developed a way (actually many, many ways) of distributing seeds further afield onto fresh, unexploited ground. Some seeds just drop to the ground and stay where they fall. Some are designed to be lifted by the wind, like the feather-light clocks of dandelions and thistle-down or the winged seeds of maples and limes. Some are designed to be transported by animals, either internally or externally.

Many seeds are packaged in a tasty coat designed to be eaten, processed in the gut and then deposited in a handy dollop of nutritious moist manure. The seeds generally pass through the animal's stomach unaffected. Some, indeed, have refined the process; mistletoe berries are rendered sticky by the passage through a bird's digestive system and are irritatingly difficult to get rid of when they emerge from the rear of the bird, necessitating him wiping the sticky faeces onto the branch of the tree. Stuck fast, the now viable seed can continue its parasitic life cycle, having been pasted in exactly the right place.

Animal dispersal
Sandbur
Beggar-ticks
Blackberry
Wind dispersal
Milkweed
Dandelion
Maple

Water dispersal

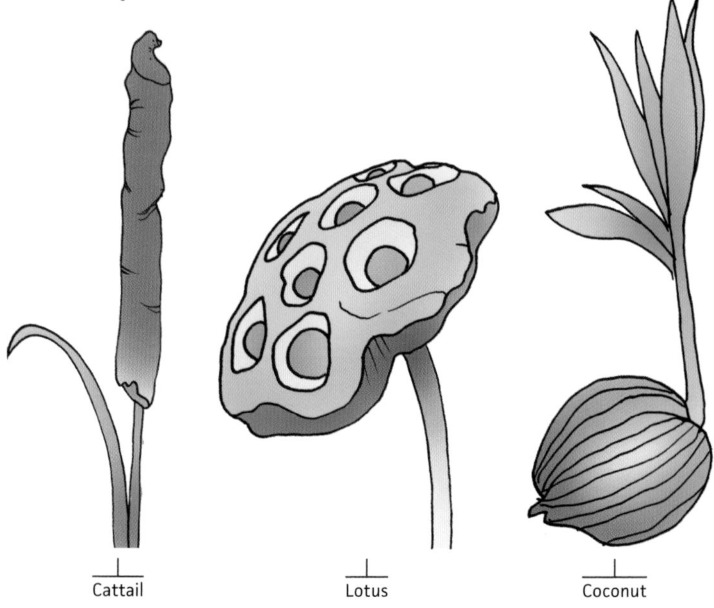

Explosion dispersal

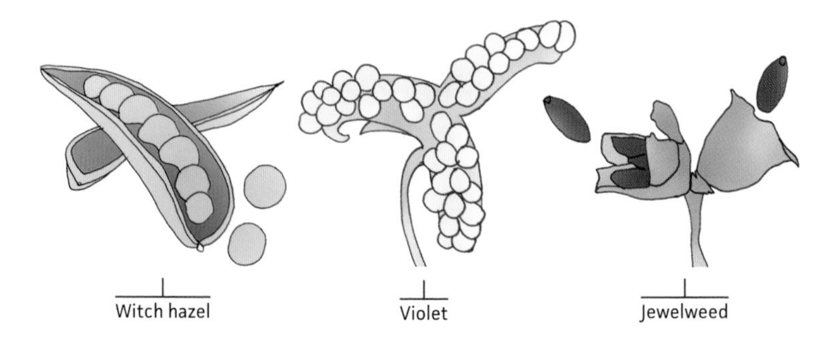

Burdock, *Arctium spp*, Cocklebur, *Xanthium spp* and cleavers, *Galium aparine*, are classic examples of seeds that are designed to stick to animal coats, later to be groomed out and deposited on new ground. What most of these seeds have in common are a coating of hooked hairs or bristles that attach themselves to the coats of passing animals.

After returning from a walk one day Swiss inventor George de Mestral's clothes were studded with burs. Before removing the burs he studied them under his magnifying glass and discovered the hooks of the burs were securely attached to the loops of the cloth. Monsieur de Mestral borrowed the idea and went on to invent Velcro!

Insects also have a role to play in seed dispersal. Myrmecochory is dispersal by ants. The ants and the plants have a symbiotic relationship whereby the ants collect the seed with its nutritious fleshy coat and take it to their nests. Having feasted on the tasty treat the ants remove the seed and deposit it in their waste area. There, among the composting frass and dead bodies, the seed germinates and begins to grow.

Many plants are packaged in a waterproof case, ready to be carried away on tides or currents. Many species of tough impermeable drift seeds can travel hundreds of miles on ocean currents before colonising new shores. Other seeds, particularly those from aquatic species, are furnished with a small air-filled pericarp, or seed-coat, to help them float. Even some desert plants rely on the rare flash flood to carry them to new ground and once there, they must endure several years of weathering in the hot, arid desert before their extremely tough coat is breeched.

Some seeds are violently expelled from the parental neighbourhood by exploding seed capsules in a method called "ballistic dispersal". Indian balsam, *Impatiens balsamina*, ejects its seeds when a touch trigger releases the cocked flower parts. The sub-tropical squirting cucumber ejects its ripe seed by means of pressure release. As the ovary fills with fluid, the pressure on the pod increases until it becomes too much and the seed-containing fluid is ejected as much as 20 feet (six metres) from the mother plant. Perhaps the most impressive ballistic dispersal is the 60 metre tall sandbox tree, *Hura crepitans*, which is able to propel its seeds, accompanied by an explosive crack, 600 feet, (45 metres) away from the parent. The woody seeds are propelled with such force that injury to people and animals isn't unusual.

The smallest seeds, the almost invisible, dust-like seeds of some orchids, contain virtually no protective or nutrient value and the seed must engage almost immediately in a partnership with certain mycorrhizal fungi in order to germinate and grow. Left to themselves they would all perish. In contrast the largest seed in the world is the Coco de Mer, the product of a palm that now survives nowhere but the Seychelles. This monster can reach a whopping 44 pounds and measures three feet in circumference and it can take up to seven years to mature plus another two years to germinate.

Peanuts
The Genuflecting Legume

A plant that does things rather differently is the peanut, which, instead of trying to disperse its seeds far and wide, deliberately plants them right in its own shadow. Peanuts are annuals, a factor which may contribute to its curious habit, as any successful seedling will not have to compete with its mother plant for light or food. Another factor may be that peanuts are legumes (hence *pea*nut) so they are able to harvest their own nitrogen from the air, thereby avoiding the risk of nitrogen depletion when grown continuously in the same place.

The seed grows into a small bushy plant which produces flowers that are self-pollinating. As each flower matures, the flower stalk, the pedicel, bends carefully and deliberately down and pushes the fertilised ovary into the soil, planting it snugly into the ground. Once planted the ovary continues to develop into a two-seeded pod which matures into what we recognise as a peanut.

It is possible to grow peanuts as a garden plant simply by planting raw shop-bought peanuts two inches deep and eight inches apart, directly into the ground in warm areas. In cooler climates plant the seeds into a pot of good garden soil a month or so before your area is frost-free, and then transplant them into the garden. Keep your crop watered and harvest after about 135 days, when the plants start to wilt. Simply pull the plant up, then dry it in the sun for a few days before roasting the nuts in a cool oven.

Fruit

A fruit is the part of a plant which contains seeds

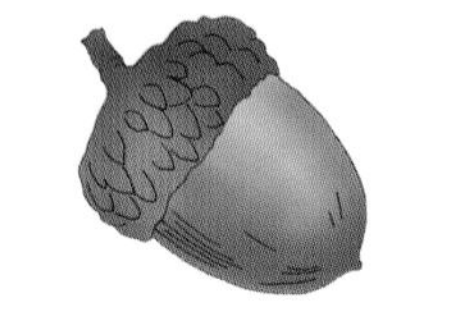

Acorn
(Oak)

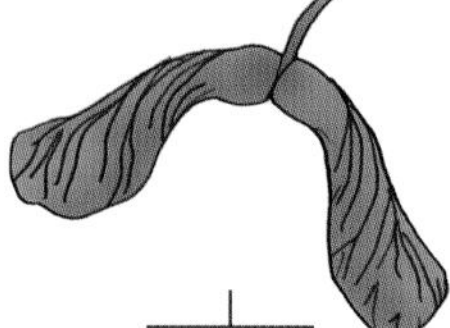

Schizocarp
(Maple)

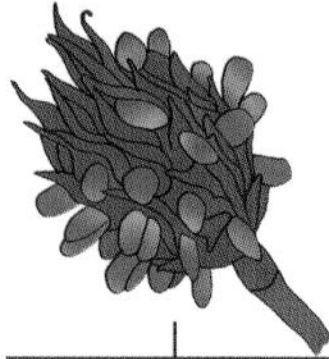

Aggregate of Follicles
(Magnolia)

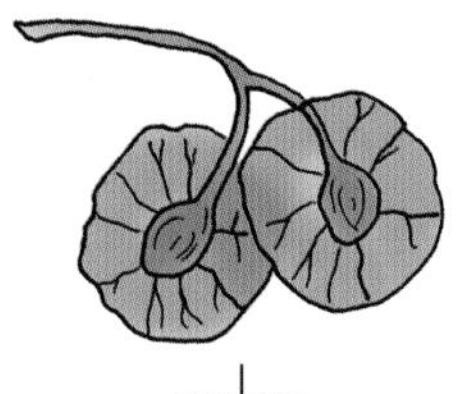

Samara
(Elm)

Aggregate of achenes
(Strawberry)

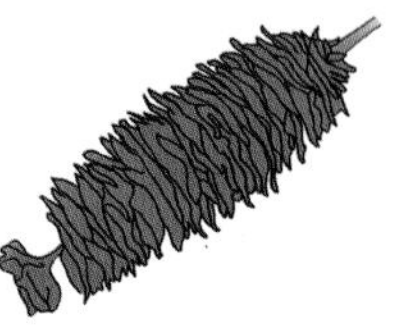

Strobile: winged Nutlet
(Birch)

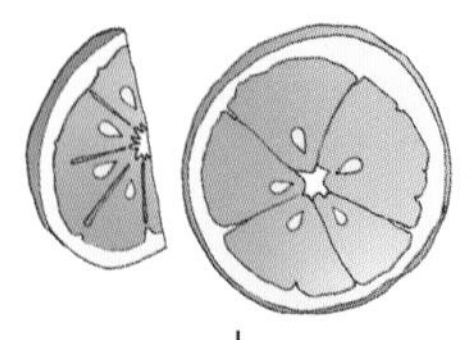

Hesperedium
(Orange, Lemon, Grapefruit)

Nutlet
(Hornbeam)

Legume (pod)
(Pea, Bean)

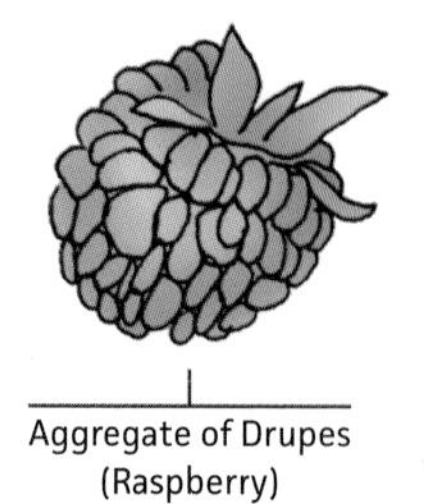

Aggregate of Drupes
(Raspberry)

Samara
(Ash)

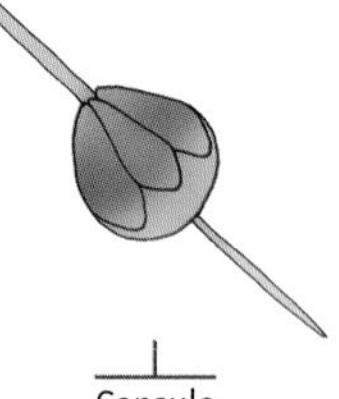

Capsule
(Forsythia, Rhododendron, Kalmia)

and these come in many curious shapes and sizes.

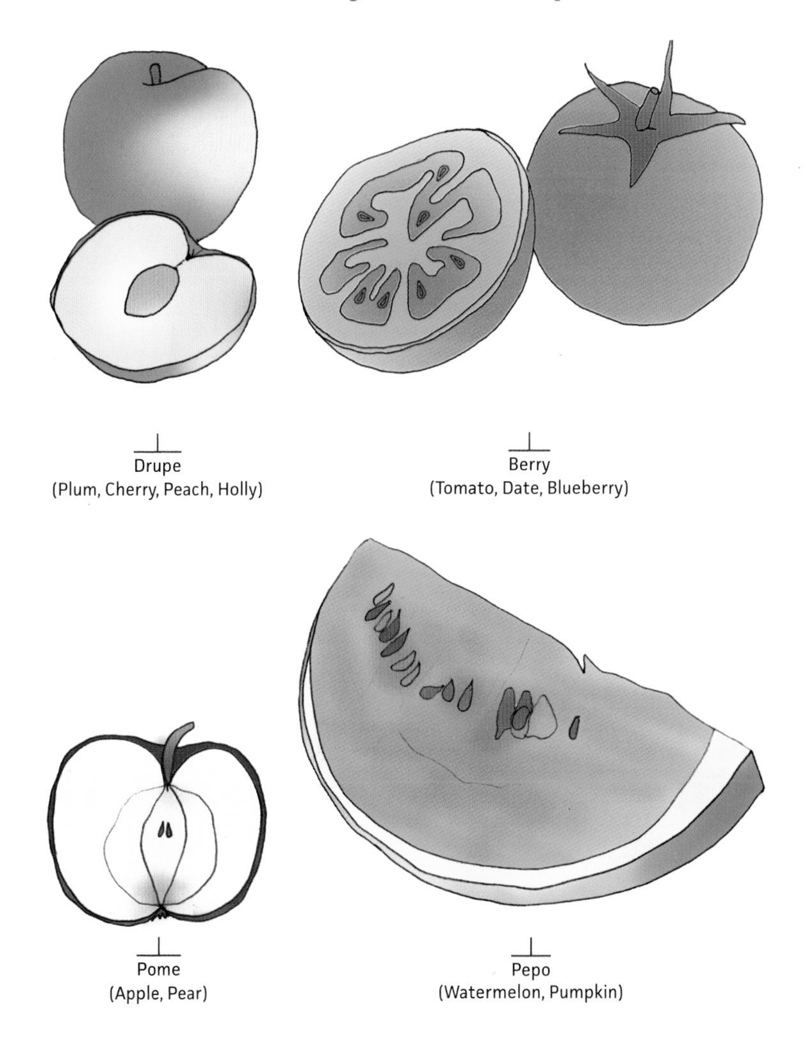

Germination

Some seeds can remain viable for several hundred years, some are relatively short-lived, lasting for only a few months while others must be sown while they are still fresh.

Seed dormancy can be controlled by light levels or by periods of very low or very high temperatures. Some seeds require their coats to be breached in order for specific moisture or oxygen levels to reach the embryo. Breaching may be achieved by the seed passing through an animal's gut or by mechanical injury. Chemical growth inhibitors may be contained within the seed coat or within the embryo plant itself, and may need to be leached away before the seed can germinate. All these factors serve to delay germination until conditions are just right for sustained growth or to stagger germination so that all seeds don't germinate at one time, allowing the population as a whole the best chance of survival.

Bluebells, for instance, need a long warm spell followed by cooler conditions to tell them that autumn has arrived and it is safe to send out roots in preparation for a head start in spring. Cycad and orchid seeds will die if they are allowed to dry out. The seed of the parasitic Witchweed must have the good fortune to land within three to four millimetres of the root of the plant that it will live off for the rest of its life as it requires the stimulation of chemicals exuded by the plant roots. Once germinated, the seed must then reach the concentrated source of the chemical within its maximum growth range of four millimetres or it will perish. The computations and permutations of light, moisture, temperature and chemical signals is mind boggling.

But at last, when the time is right and conditions are suitable, water penetrates the seed coat and is absorbed by the embryonic root (called the radicle) which swells, breaks through the coat then pushes down through the soil. The little embryo, imbibing strength from its endosperm, pushes a shoot upwards, either thrusting straight up through the soil or bending up with a hooked stem, later to straighten and grow up towards the light.

Some seeds can remain viable for several hundred years; the record is currently held by the seeds of the Judean Date palm, found in an urn in Herod the Great's Palace in Israel, which remain viable after an impressive 2,000 years.

Sometimes the real challenge is to stop seeds from germinating, and to preserve them as viable specimens for as long as possible. The Millennium Seed Bank in West Sussex, UK, is the largest in the world and together with other ground-breaking institutions is attempting to preserve seeds before they become extinct in the wild.

Ten per cent of the world's wild species have now been collected and saved in the Millennium Seed Bank and the aim for 2020 is to increase that to 25 per cent.

Leaves

Leaves, it could be argued, are at the heart of what makes a plant a plant. They are where photosynthesis takes place, they are, usually, green. They are the biggest identification feature of most plants and learning how to look at them and to understand them from the inside out is a great pleasure.

There are three distinct tissue layers in the leaves of most plants; the epidermis, the mesophyll and the vascular bundles or veins which transport water, sugars and nutrients around the leaf. The *epidermis*, the skin of the leaf, is covered by a waxy cuticle which protects the leaf from insects and other pests. On the undersides of the leaf are pores called stoma which act as the breathing holes of the leaf and of the plant as a whole. Carbon dioxide is taken in through the stoma and oxygen and water vapour are expelled. Plants can control the passage of these gases by opening and closing their stoma at will. The *mesophyll*, the middle bit, is where most of the chloroplasts are found and where all the hard work of photosynthesis happens.

While there are small veins, the vascular bundles distributed throughout the leaf, the main leaf vein acts like an artery, transporting food and water to the smaller veins. Within the vascular bundles the xylem tissue carries its nutrient-rich water up from the roots and around the plant and it is located towards the upper sides of the leaf. The phloem tissue, transporting its sweet river of sugary water down to the roots, is oriented towards the underside of the leaf. That is why aphids and other piercing and sucking bugs congregate underneath the leaf.

Leaves are little oxygen and sugar factories; they keep plants—and us—alive.

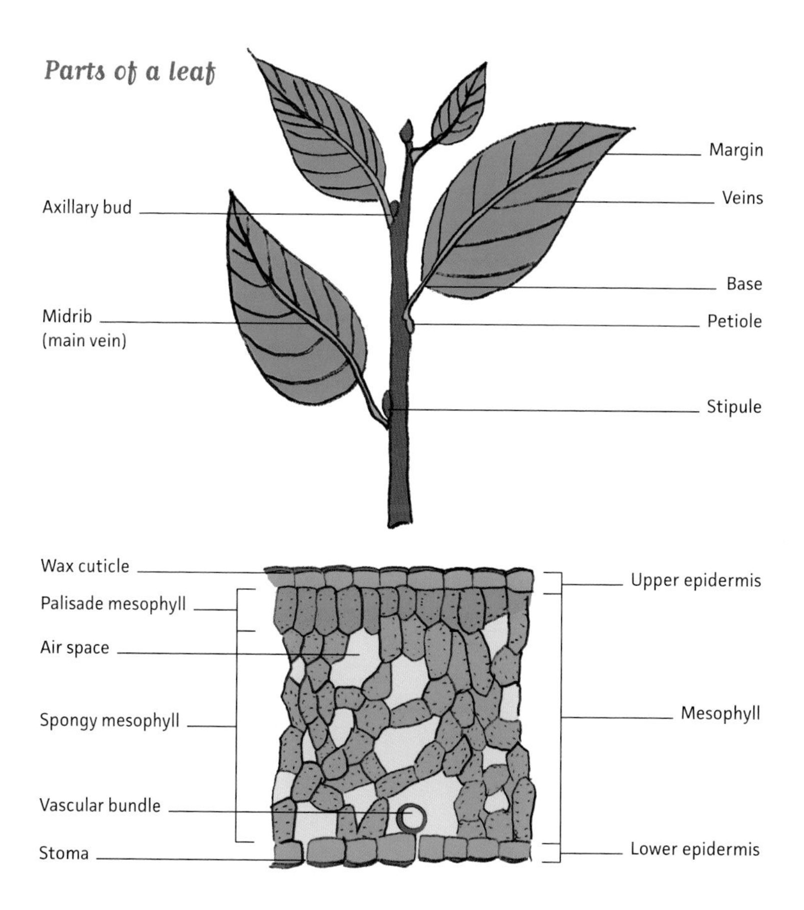

Carnivorous plants often have leaves that have been modified to act as traps. These plants live in areas that are very poor in nutrients where the soil doesn't contain everything the plant needs to survive. Instead the plant supplements its diet with a selection of tasty, nutrient-rich insects (and in some cases amphibians or small mammals). The Venus flytrap, that gruesome and fascinating curiosity loved by little boys, has one of the fastest movements in the plant world. Once the trigger hairs are touched twice the two sides of the leaf snap shut along the midrib in under half a second, trapping the unfortunate fly inside. Logically as these traps—despite being so showy—are simply modified leaves, the Venus flytrap also produces very pretty flowers held high above the grisly dining table.

Photosynthesis

The conversion of solar energy into chemical energy.

Leaves are the food factories of plants. They are the primary source of a plant's energy as they are able to manufacture sugars in the form of carbohydrates with the aid of carbon dioxide from the air and water absorbed through the roots with the aid of chlorophyll, the green pigment in the leaves. As a by-product, oxygen is made and expelled through the stoma, the little holes on the under surface of the leaf.

If that all sounds a bit too simple, there is a rather more detailed version of photosynthesis. You first have to think of a leaf as a sort of Russian doll. In the leaf are cells and in those cells are organelles (small organs), in the organelles are chloroplasts and in the chloroplasts are thylakoids and in the thylakoids are chlorophyll molecules. It is the chlorophyll molecules that are able to capture the sun's energy.

The first part of photosynthesis is called the "light dependent reaction" because it needs light to work. It also needs water and carbon dioxide which are already present in the plant, along with other substances such as plant enzymes. In the light reaction the sunlight causes the water to split into its basic components of hydrogen and oxygen. The oxygen is released into the atmosphere through the stoma, and the hydrogen, with help from leaf enzymes, combines with the carbon dioxide to form a substance called ATP. This is used in the next step in photosynthesis.

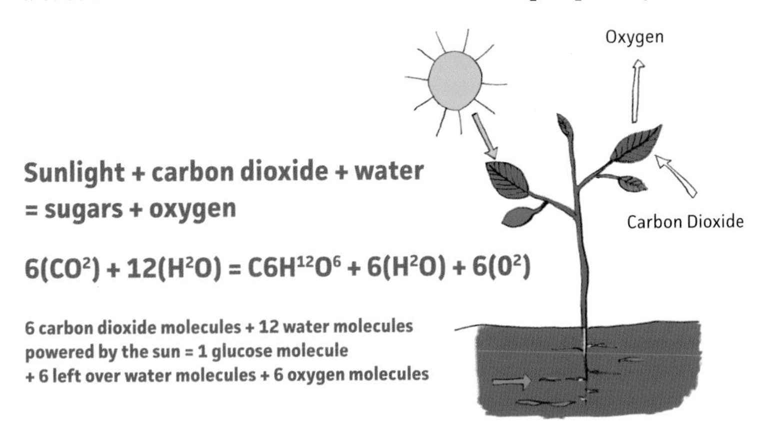

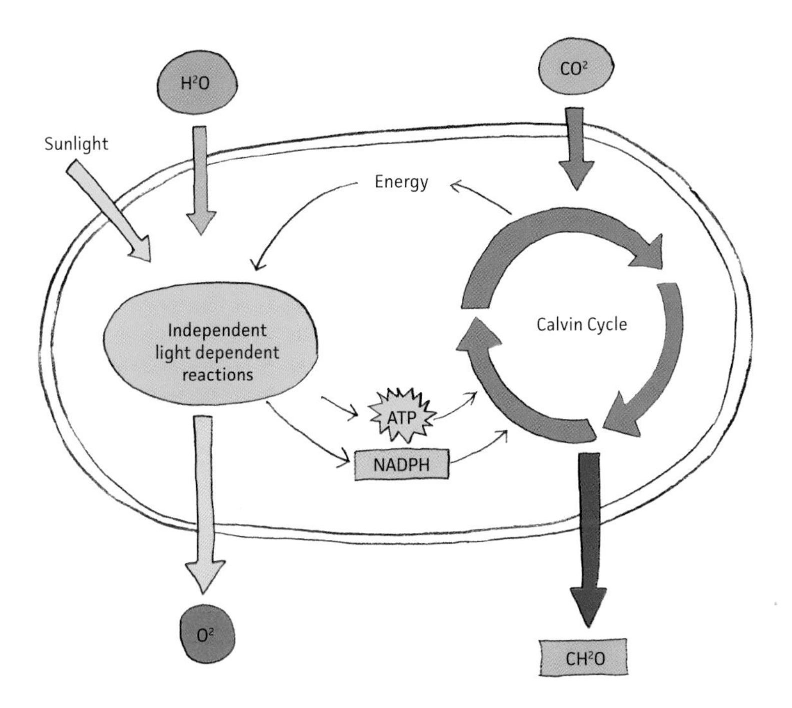

The second part of photosynthesis is called the "light independent" reaction and is also known as the Calvin Cycle. In the cycle three carbon dioxide molecules join up with three 5-carbon molecules to make three new molecules. Then an enzyme splits each of these three new molecules in two to make six new molecules, each containing three carbons. One of these changes into glucose (the plant's food), and the other five are rearranged to form three 5-carbon molecule… and then the cycle begins again.

There is an exception to every rule and one of these is the rather charming little green sea slug, *Elysia chlorotica*. He is not a plant, nor does he pretend to be one, although he does have one thing very much in common with the plant world. He appears to be the only animal which is able to run on solar energy. Scientists have discovered that not only does *E. chlorotica* steal and store chloroplasts from the algae on which it feeds, it also ingests the gene needed to maintain the chloroplasts in working order and then incorporates the gene into its own cells. Having furnished itself with all the machinery needed to run on solar power it is then able to survive with only the sun for nourishment.

Abscission

As the days shorten and the nights grow colder, trees begin to change colour. The most breathtaking colours are produced when the days are warm and sunny and the nights are cold and crisp.

The green pigment, chlorophyll, is the main colourant of leaves throughout much of the year. Chlorophyll is essential in the process of photosynthesis. While the leaf is growing chlorophyll is constantly being broken down, used up and replaced by the plant.

Other pigments are also present to a greater or lesser degree but it isn't until the days grow shorter that chlorophyll production decreases and the other colours begin to shine through. Anthocyanins are light reactive, so the sunnier it is, the stronger the colour; they also react to soil pH, the colour travelling from reds through purples and up towards the blue spectrum as the pH rises. Carotenoids, the pigment responsible for clear yellows and oranges in leaves (as well as in carrots) don't react to pH. They are present in the leaf all the time, but are masked by the green of the chlorophyll. Tannin, present in oaks and beech, are also responsible for some of the glowing coppers and browns of certain trees.

Just as the colours reach their flaming best the show comes to an end. The plant is shutting down to cope with a challenging season of very cold or dry weather. The veins that carry nutrients and sugars into and out of the leaves begin to shut down and sugars move out of the leaf for storage in the branches and roots. At the point where the leaf joins the stem a layer of cork cells called an abscission zone begins to form. Pectic acid turns into pectin, the cells weaken, the winds blow and the leaf falls.

In the average garden there may not be room for sugar maples and trembling aspens, but there are still plenty of smaller plants that offer a glorious palette of reds, golds and purples to illuminate the autumn garden. *Euonymus* Red Cascade, *Cornus* Mid-winter Fire and many other dogwoods, *Rhus typhina*, *Cercis canadensis* Forest Pansy and *Cotinus coggygria* will all set the garden alight.

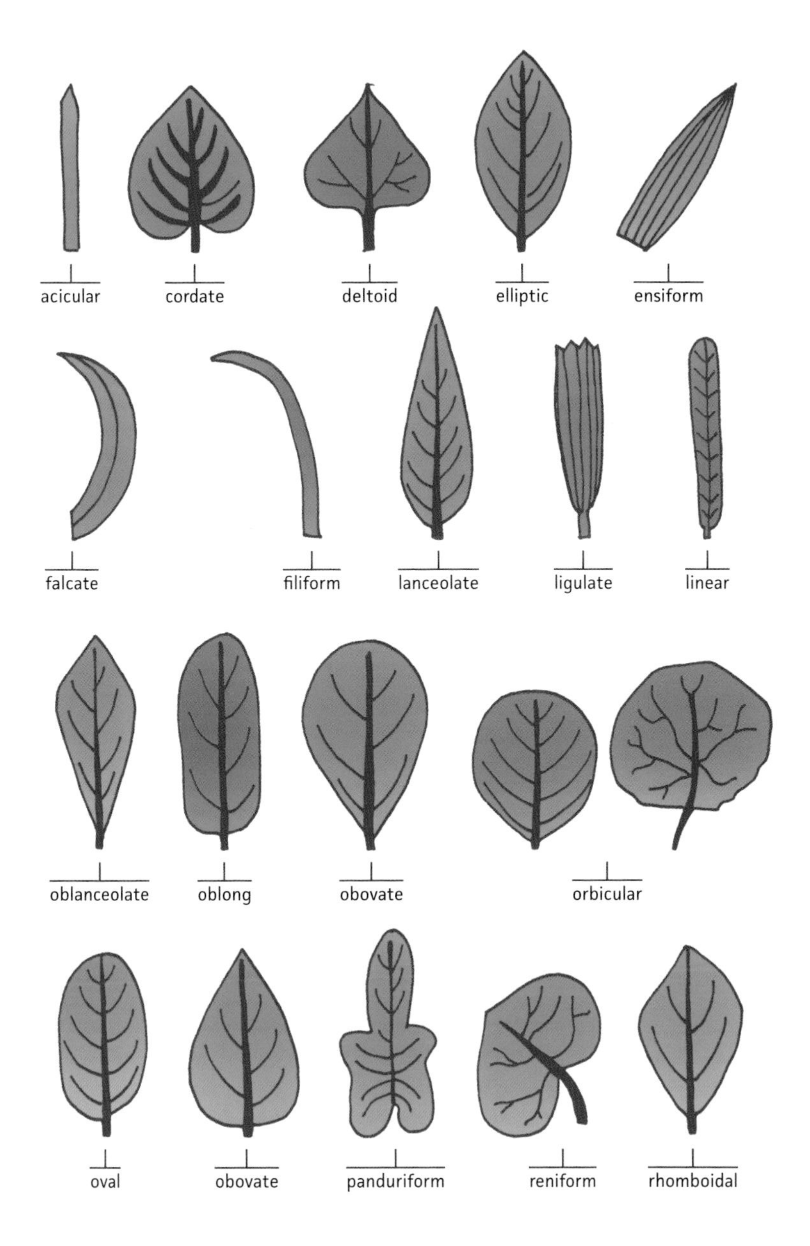
acicular
cordate
deltoid
elliptic
ensiform
falcate
filiform
lanceolate
ligulate
linear
oblanceolate
oblong
obovate
orbicular
oval
obovate
panduriform
reniform
rhomboidal

Roots

Roots come in all shapes and sizes. The obvious purpose of any root is to provide anchorage and to absorb water and nutrients from the soil. Another job, a very important one, is that roots are designed to store energy in the form of starches and sugars. Think of the sweet starchy roots of potatoes and carrots.

Roots arising from anywhere on the plant other than from another root are called "adventitious". Adventitious roots grow from the nodes of strawberries, from stem tips of periwinkle and from the upright stems of corn. Huge aerial roots, prop roots, grow down major limbs of tropical trees that grow in shallow soils. Some plants are so inclined to root that severed leaves, like those of begonia and African violet, stems of plants like mint and entire branches of willow, will root simply by being placed in water or in contact with damp soil.

Roots are not always as they seem… tubers, corms, bulbs and rhizomes are all modifications of different parts of plants that do the work of roots —support, energy or water storage—in different ways.

Roots also undertake a vitally important role in the ecology of the planet as it is in the roots that relationships are made and broken, bargaining and even cheating is commonplace. Without roots and the partnerships they forge with soil organisms there would be no nutrients to transport around the plant. Think fungi, think bacteria. Think peas and beans.

Leaves supply energy but do not supply nutrients. For that you need roots.

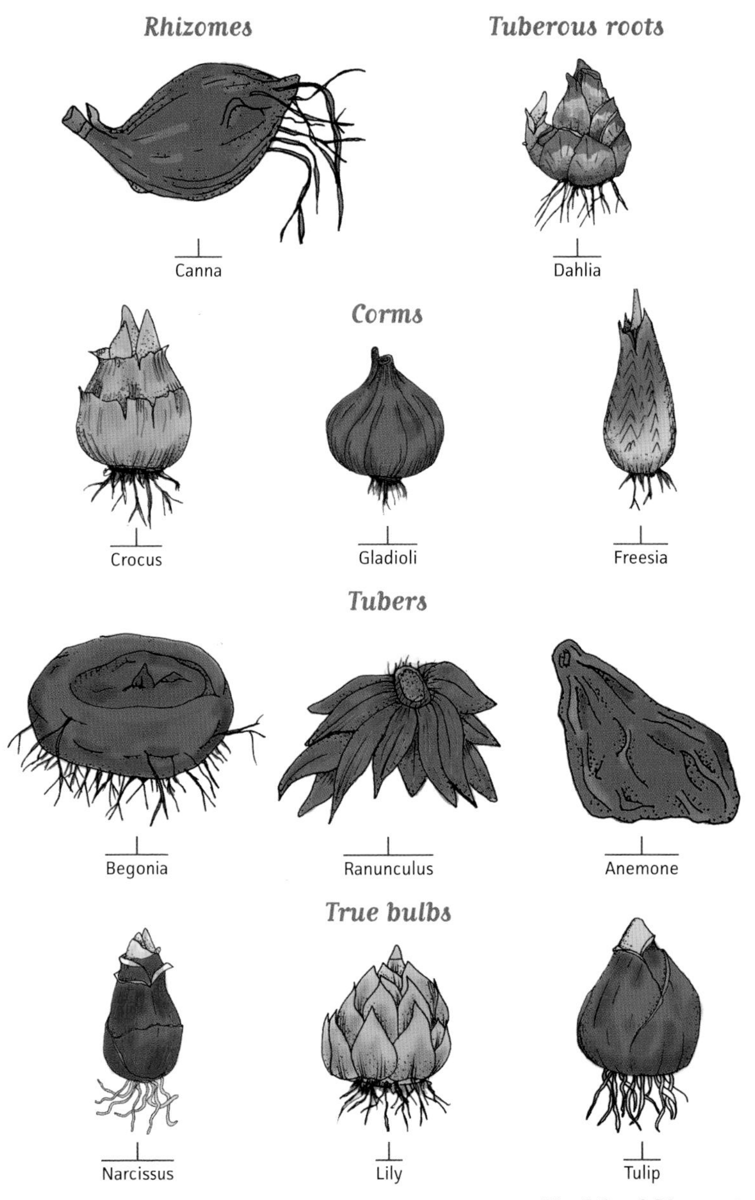
Rhizomes
Tuberous roots
Canna
Dahlia
Corms
Crocus
Gladioli
Freesia
Tubers
Begonia
Ranunculus
Anemone
True bulbs
Narcissus
Lily
Tulip

In the Rhizosphere

In the soil of your garden, under fields and in the woods, plant roots form symbiotic partnerships with various types of fungi and bacteria. The more we know about soil organisms the more importance they assume in soil management. The basics for the understanding of the interaction of fungi and plants is that, while plants can make carbohydrates through photosynthesis, fungi cannot. And while fungi, in their microscopic grinding and dissolving of rock and soil fragments, can synthesise phosphates, nitrogen and other essential nutrients, they are completely unable to make carbohydrates as they lack chlorophyll and the ability to photosynthesise. The thin fungal threads, called hyphae, together with the plant root cells, bond to make a mycorrhizal association where plant and fungi exchange the substances they need to survive. More fascinating still is that this relationship is not singular, nor mutually exclusive. The hyphae links a whole community of plants in a crazy, constantly shifting exchange and trade of carbohydrates, water and nutrients. Low level shrubs that are starved of light by the tall trees above receive a supplement of carbon through the hyphae link. Cheaters, either plant or fungal, are punished by their partners through reduced amounts of carbon or nutrient exchange. If the plant community dies, so does the fungal community, and visa versa.

Now you can go to the garden centre and buy a box of fungi to add to the planting hole when you plant your roses, and when depleted areas of forest are replanted, great emphasis is placed not only on planting trees but on re-introducing fungal hyphae at the same time. It is now recognised that to maintain a healthy ecosystem the less the soil is damaged the better it will perform, and this is the basis for the trend in forest gardening and permaculture. Double digging is out.

Plants from the legume family (*Fabacea*) which include beans, peas, alfalfa and lupins, are well known for their ability to fix nitrogen in the soil. However, it is not the plants that fix the nitrogen, but their guests. Nitrogen, is unavailable to plants in its natural state so while it is the most common chemical in the atmosphere, in order for plants to use it, nitrogen must first be converted into a chemical form that can be taken up by plant roots. Here is where the legumes come in. Legumes and some other plants form a mutually beneficial relationship with several species of rhizobia, a bacteria which is able to trap and convert nitrogen into a usable state. Rhizobia take up residence in the nodules on the plant roots and trap, convert and supply nitrogen to their hosts while the plants happily supply their guests with carbohydrates in the form of sugars. To make the most of the available nitrogen a gardener would have to dig the plant into the soil at the height of flowering when the most nitrogen is stored in the nodules. After this the nitrogen level falls dramatically.

We tend to look on plants from the legume family as rather benevolent beings, almost as if they are bestowing on us a gift of nitrogen fixation. The truth is that they are even more reliant on the rhizobia than we are. Legumes planted in sterilised soil, with no existing soil rhizobia to harness, will soon grow yellow and die of a nitrogen deficiency.

Some plants are more obviously dependent on their relationship with fungi than others but around 80 per cent of the plants tested so far have some sort of mutually beneficial bond with the fungi that live in the soil around their roots (the rhizosphere). In most cases the plants transfer carbon that they have made through photosynthesis to the fungi in return for nutrients. Fascinatingly, in some groups of orchids that grow in such low light levels that they are unable to photosynthesise, the fungi have taken on the task of transferring not only nutrients to their orchid partners, but carbon as well. This type of fungi forms a symbiotic relationship with nearby trees, collects carbon from them (in return for nutrients) keeps some carbon for itself and passes the rest on to the orchid... although studies continue, it is thought that in this case the non-photosynthetic orchid is cheating, giving nothing back in return for the carbon (carbohydrates) that it receives. This community exchange of water, minerals, nutrients and carbon has been demonstrated, in some cases to cover areas of hundreds of square miles.

Stem

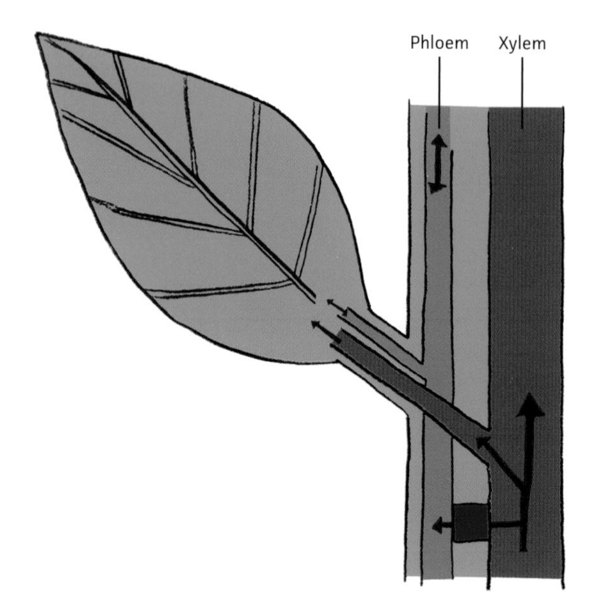

The stem acts to support the plant above the ground and helps it to reach for the light. It is also the main body of the plant. Stems can act as food storage organs like crocus corms or the rhizomes of iris or ginger, photosynthetic organs such as the flattened, thorny modified stems of butcher's broom or climbing organs such as the tendrils of ivy or the twining stems of runner beans. Whether a stem belongs to a geranium or a mighty pine tree, the function is the same.

For the plant to survive it must be able to transport water upwards from the roots and move carbohydrates in the form of sugars downwards from the leaves. It does this neat exchange in the vascular system. The vascular system, the veins of the plant, is primarily made up of two types of tissue: phloem and xylem.

The best known and recognised xylem tissue is wood. Elongated xylem cells arranged end to end in a tube formation die, leaving the hardened cell wall behind to make the pipe that zips the nutrients up the trunk and around the plant. Xylem cells are easily recognised in the cross-section of a tree trunk as the dark rings of late summer growth. In trees the xylem, as it dies, forms the inner wood of the tree. The phloem, as it dies, joins the bark and is sloughed away.

The mineral rich water in the xylem travels up through the plant under transpirational pressure. Transpiration is the action whereby water is drawn up through the plant and out of the stoma—the pores—in the leaves, where it evaporates.

The fluid in the phloem flows down and around the plant taking food, the sugars that have been formed during photosynthesis, down to the roots.

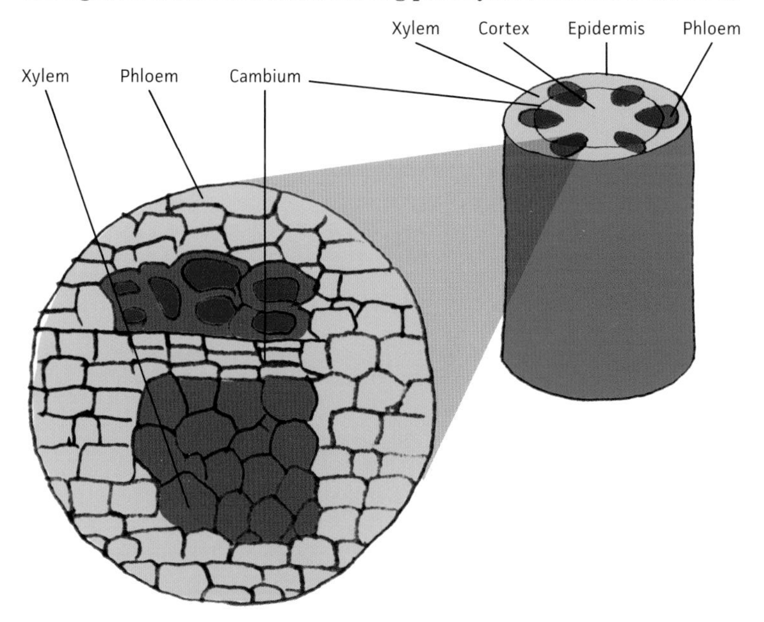

Stems are probably the most economically versatile of plant organs. Stems, trunks, sap, bark and extracts from all of these are sources of items and substances which play a part in our everyday lives; potatoes are modified stems, kohlrabi are swollen stem bases, asparagus, sugarcane, cinnamon, cellulose, maple sugar, quinine, chicle (the main ingredient of chewing gum), tannins, cork, rubber, resin, turpentine, bamboo and rattan are all derived from plant stems. And of course there is wood and paper. And this is just the quick list.

Dendrochronology
A Window Into History

Dendrochronology is the science of dating trees, living or dead, by counting the annual rings. Trees in temperate zones grow one ring every year. In the spring, when conditions are usually favourable and rainfall is plentiful, layer upon layer of large cells are laid down, increasing the diameter of the tree. In the less favourable months of late summer cells are added more slowly. These cells are smaller and darker. One annual ring is composed of a ring of early wood and a ring of late wood.

The pattern of annual tree-rings changes each year, depending on the growing conditions at the time. In good conditions a tree will grow well and produce a thick ring. Under poor conditions the ring will be thinner.

These patterns can be compared and matched, ring for ring, with trees growing in the same geographical zone under similar conditions and the study of these rings builds up a database for a particular area from which weather patterns and events can be deciphered.

Conditions in the immediate neighbourhood can also be deciphered by the way the rings are formed across the plane. For example, narrow rings for more than three years indicates that the tree was being crowded by neighbours, while scars in the tree rings hold clues to fire damage or insect infestation. Being able to read tree rings is like reading a history book.

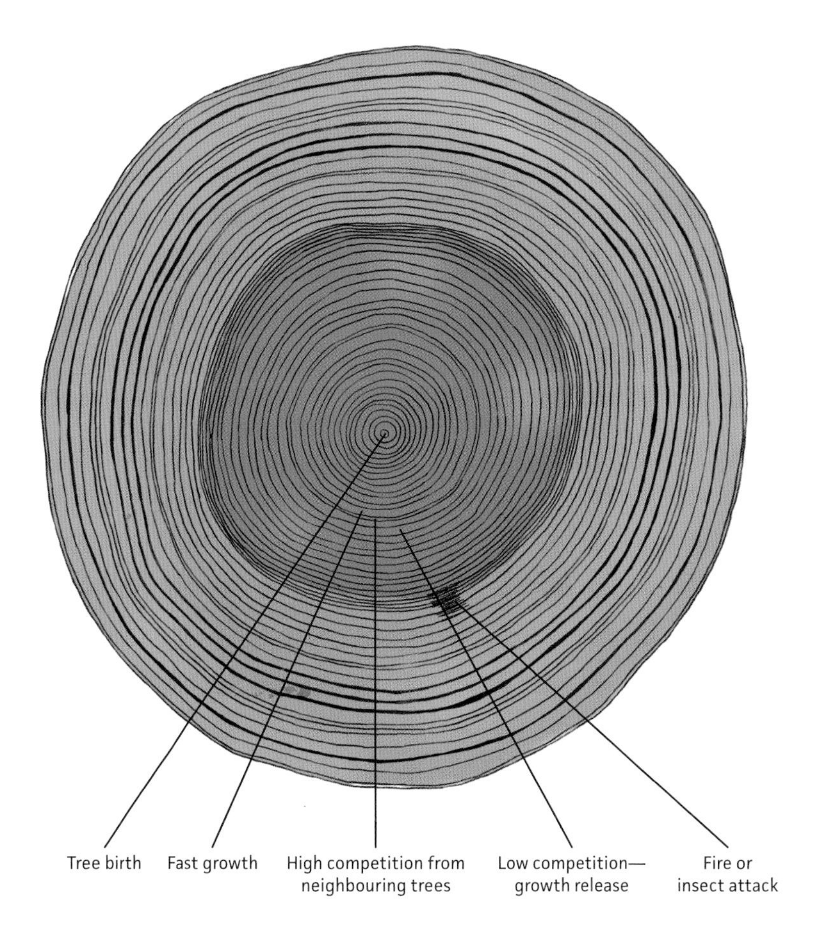
Tree birth
Fast growth
High competition from neighbouring trees
Low competition—growth release
Fire or insect attack

Twigs

Twigs are a wonderful key to identifying winter shrubs and trees. Dormant trees can be quite easily identified by taking a close look at the twigs and buds. Notice the position of the buds on the twig, the shape and size of the buds and the markings on the twig itself. Some twigs can be identified at a distance, but others offer a bit more of a challenge.

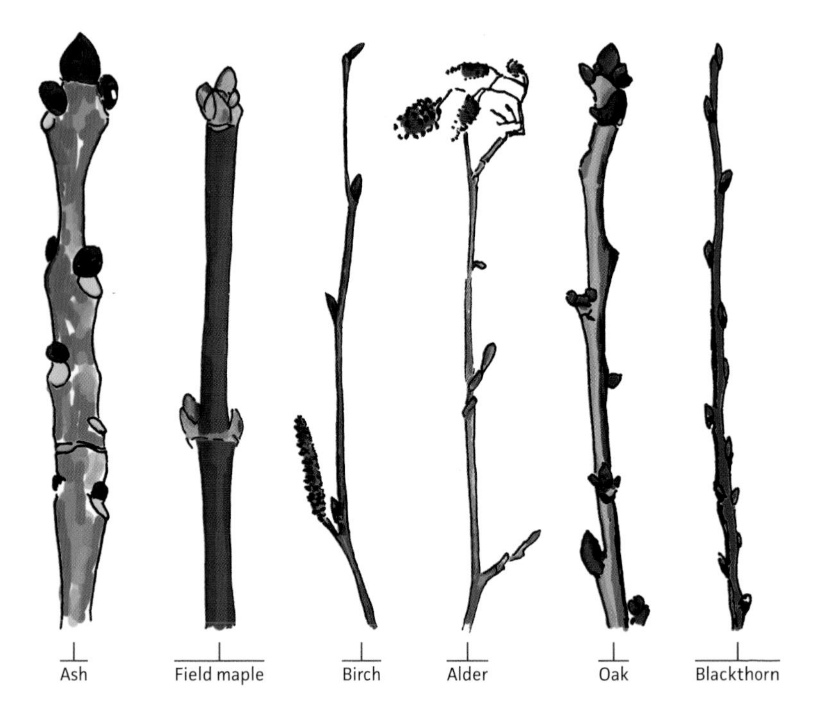

Lime
Dog rose
Elm
Beech
Rowan
Lilac
Larch
Sycamore
Horse chestnut
Hazel

Allelopathy
Chemical Warfare by Plants

Allelon = each
Pathos = suffering

Black walnuts are the classic example of allelopathy. For thousands of years people have recognised that few plants grow beneath walnut trees. At first glance it could be assumed that it was too dry, or shady for anything to grow but in fact the tree is deliberately poisoning the plants that trespass on its patch in all sorts of ingenious ways.

Allelopathic chemicals can occur in any part of a plant and may inhibit competition by changing the chemical nature of the soil, by raising the pH, inhibiting the ability of plants to germinate or to take up nutrients, or by interfering with the essential symbiotic relationships between plants and the fungi in the soil.

Spotted knapweed, *Centaurea maculosa*, produces a herbicide from its roots that kills off the competition by assisting the release of toxic levels of phosphorus in the surrounding soil. Garlic mustard, *Allaria petiolata*, produces chemicals that suppress the mychorrhizal fungi that live symbiotically with competing plants; the partnership is broken; the competing plants weaken and die.

Allelopathy can be exploited in gardening by planting cover crops that have short term allelopathic effects. Winter rye, for example, suppresses pigweeds, lambsquarters, purslane, and crabgrass. Sunflower inhibits the growth of morning glories. Tomatoes and other members of the *Solanacea* family thrive when transplanted through recently-killed residues of rye. Winter grain cover crop residues have been reported to reduce growth of cabbage, but to stimulate peas, beans, and cucumbers.

If the cover crop is cut and forked-in to the top inch or two of soil, the effect of the chemicals is quite short lived, and will suppress the germination of small seeded weeds and crops such as lettuce. However if the residue is left on the top of the soil the effect persists for longer and will stop germination in the top one inch of soil for up to ten weeks—this can prove very useful in areas where vegetables are transplanted rather than sown from seed or if deeply sown, large-seeded vegetables such as squash or beans are chosen.

Endophytes

Are organisms—bacteria or fungi—that live within plants and often offer some protection from attack by herbivores, as well as increasing the plant's ability to tolerate drought and other challenging conditions. An interesting side effect of endophyte infection is that the endophytes themselves may be beneficial in their own right: the cancer drug taxol is sourced from endophyte infected yew plant.

Thigmonastic movements

Are rapid defensive movements in response to touch. The sensitive plant *Mimosa pudica*, and wood sorrel, *Oxalis spp*, quickly close their leaves when touched which startles and deters attack by predators.

Chemical warfare

Some chemical compounds are selective in that they inhibit the growth of some plants but stimulate the growth of others. Allelopathic chemicals tend to be species specific in that they often affect one species of plant, but have no effect on another.

Mutualism

Some plants release volatile oils when attacked which attract the predators which feed on the herbivores that feed on the plants. The chemical reaction triggered by a pine sawfly laying her eggs on a pine tree triggers the tree to produce volatile oils. These oils attract parasitic wasps and flies which fly in to feed on the pests.

Ants

Ants are often employed by plants to protect them against herbivores. In return the plant provides housing within the structure of the plant (in hollow thorns or stems) and often lays on a buffet of nectar or fruit to keep its defenders happy .

Mimicry

Some plants avoid being chosen as a depository for insect eggs by pretending to already be playing host to a clutch of eggs. Passionflowers try and avoid the cannibalistic Heliconius butterflies laying eggs on their leaves by producing nectaries that look like mature Heliconius eggs.

Mechanical defense

May come in the form of armour, hairs, prickles, spines or thorns. Waxy cuticles, resins and sap can all offer irritant defenses. Hard seed coats and tough coatings hinder or halt attacks by herbivores.

Gardening

Life Cycles

Annuals

Annuals have a life cycle of just one year and in that year they will germinate, grow to maturity, flower, seed and die. Some annuals need a very early start in the year in order to flower. Some perennials, such as the yarrow, *Achillea millefolium* and Russel hybrid lupins are treated as annuals, as they are so quick to mature.

Biennials

Biennials complete their life cycles in two years, usually germinating and developing a characteristic rosette of leaves in the first year and flowering, setting seed and dying in the second year. The ground-hugging rosette is nature's way of collecting and storing nutrients in a very energy efficient way, and one which minimises the risk of weather damage. Not all biennials need two full years to live their life, so some can be sown late in the summer of year one, to flower early in the summer of year two.

Perennials

Perennials are plants that come back year after year from the same root stock. Some species of perennial, just like some shrubs and even trees, are naturally short-lived and will enjoy an abbreviated life-span even if they are given ideal conditions. Others seem to go on forever, no matter what you do to them.

Trees

Trees, of course, are the longest living of all plants, some of them surviving for many hundreds of years. *Pinus longaeva*, the Bristlecone pines, are generally long-lived but even by their standards the specimen known affectionately as Methuselah which lives on a hilltop in California is doing rather well; trunk wood samples have dated this tree at just short of 5,000 years, its seed estimated to have taken root around 2832 BC, about the time Stonehenge was built but before the construction of the first Egyptian pyramid.

All plants have a life-expectancy that may be shortened or lengthened by the conditions in which they find themselves, so you may see the same plant referred to as an annual in northern climates and a perennial in warmer, southern conditions.

Climate & Microclimate

Hardiness is another factor that defines a plant and its life cycle. Plants are often labelled as tender, half-hardy or hardy. Keep in mind that hardiness is relative and it is best to rely on the word of a nurseryman rather than a label which might not have been designed for your area.

Hardiness has as much to do with wind, and moisture as it does with temperature. The relatively tender shrub, *Buddleia davidii* will tolerate the bitter onslaught of a Canadian winter as long as it is protected by a blanket of snow; however all the branches sticking out above the snow cover will perish. True alpines that can tolerate the bitter drying wind and snow of mountain tops will struggle in the damper and warmer winters on the valley floor. Dry, freezing winds are a large factor in winter fatalities, especially for conifers and other plants that retain their leaves throughout the colder months. If you have a favourite plant which is borderline hardy take the time to rig up a windbreak. Don't enclose your plant entirely unless you are willing to go out on unexpectedly warm winter days and open it up to stop it overheating. Simply sink three sturdy bamboos or stakes into the ground and staple or tie some hessian or burlap sacking to protect the windward side of your plant.

Winter wet can also prove more of a challenge than low temperatures. If in doubt, dig in plenty of humus, gravel, or sand, depending on the structure of your soil, in order to improve the drainage; in winter, almost anything is better than wet feet!

Microclimates are as important as the larger local climate. An unpruned shrub that is prone to fungus or bacterial attack may suffer more simply because air isn't able to circulate around the closely packed leaves. Prune out some branches to open it up a bit and you will lower humidity levels enough to remove the problem. Frost pockets are caused by colder air falling and becoming trapped in hollows or against boundaries so avoid planting tender plants in dips or dead-end corridors of the garden.

Plant Climate Zones

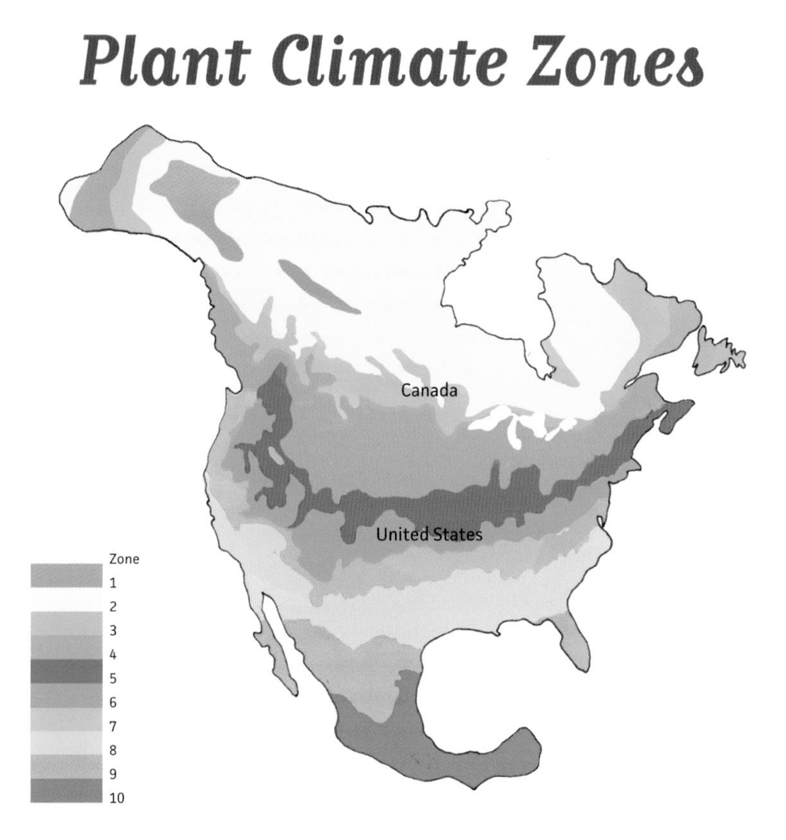

Hardiness zones were first used in North America because of the great variance of winter temperatures between the north and the south. Introduced by the US Department of Agriculture, these zones were soon adopted by Canada and then by Britain, the rest of Europe and Australia. The great advantage of this system is that it gives a quick, general guide to the lowest winter temperatures and in this era of internationally shared information, an internationally understood system is valuable. However the system does not take into account other factors, such as humidity, summer highs and lows or the protective effects of reliable snow cover.

The UK is warmed by the Gulf Stream, so that despite its northerly position—which shares the same latitude as Churchill, Canada, famous for its polar bears—northern England and some parts of northern Europe share the same hardiness zone as Texas and Florida. They do not, needless to say, enjoy the same climate, just the average winter minimums.

Because of the different extremes of the Australian climate, the Australian government has introduced its own hardiness zones which take into account annual temperatures and moisture levels of a given area.

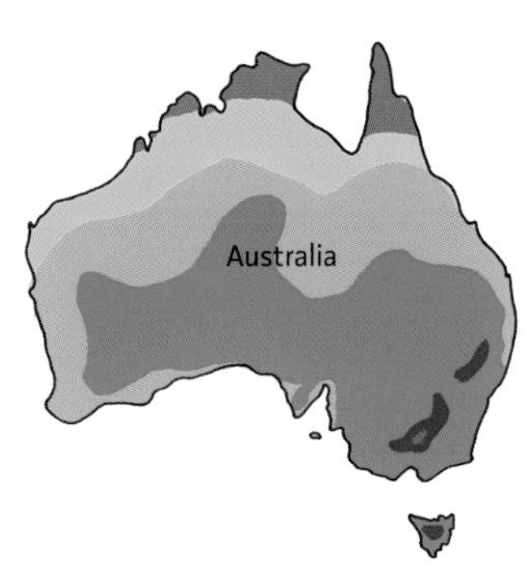

	60 to 50 F	15 to 10 C
	50 to 40 F	10 to 4 C
	40 to 30 F	4 to 1 C
	30 to 20 F	1 to 6 C
	20 to 10 F	-6 to -12 C
	10 to 0 F	-12 to -18 C

Plant Breeding

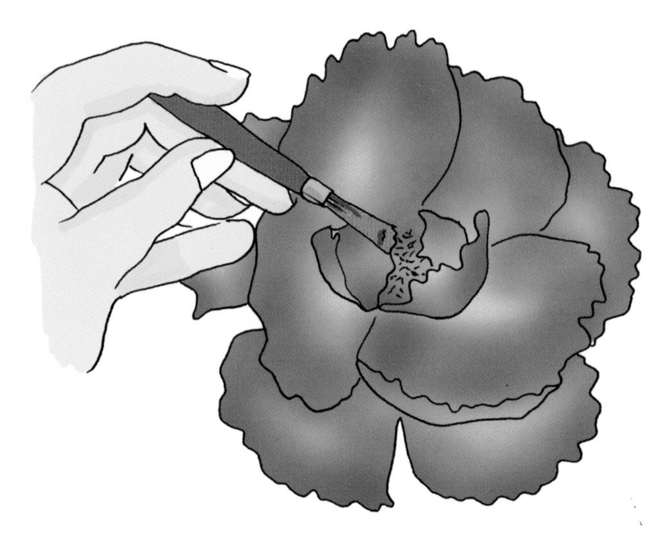

Plant breeding is big business and billions of dollars are generated every year by companies vying, for one reason or another, to come up with new varieties and cultivars. On a gardening level, seed companies are constantly searching for the next big thing. This is done by growing acres of single crops and looking out for new 'sports' or mutations as well as actively breeding new varieties by choosing parent plants with appealing characteristics. Some crops are bred and propagated using fairly traditional methods while others use genetic modification or micro-propagation, which is cloning a new plant from a single cell.

An F1 hybrid is a result of crossing two genetically different plants by harvesting pollen from one and dusting it on the stigma of the other in highly controlled conditions. The process is long and laborious. First you need to breed two populations of plants that will breed true most of the time. If for instance you were trying to breed the hypothetically elusive tall red petunia you would first need to establish two stable populations of parent plants, each having characteristics that you want; in this case the red flower and the height. In our hypothetical breeding program, there already exist tall blue petunias and short red ones, but no petunias which are both tall and red.

In isolation, begin by selecting a group of tall blue petunias and interbreed these over and over, each time weeding out any seedlings that vary greatly from the ideal—in this case discard any that are short or any colour other than blue. At the same time, in another greenhouse, choose another group of petunias, this time short and red. Breed these, as before, weeding out the misfits. To reach a stage where each of your populations breed true most of the time would take about six years. As generation follows generation, the plants in the trial will become less vigorous.

Now that you have two stable but unrelated populations of inbred plants you can attempt to cross them to achieve your ideal tall red petunia, your F1 hybrid. First ensure that no contamination can take place—you don't want pollen from over the garden fence to contaminate your trials. Remove the anthers from one population to make sure there is no unwanted pollination between red and red or blue and blue. Now take the pollen from one population and, with a paint brush, dust it onto the stigma of the other, then wait for the seed to develop, plant it up and wait to see if you have any worthwhile results.

This first generation (F1 or first filial) progeny from your cross-breeding should be uniform and will demonstrate a burst of hybrid vigour as they draw on the strengths of both parent lines. Unfortunately this breeding will only last for one generation as any further crosses will revert back to their grandparents, and will loose their uniformity and their vigour.

Although F1 hybrids have been around, commercially, for a relatively short time, the story began 200 years ago in 1787 when a wealthy English gentleman by the name of Thomas Andrew Knight changed from trying to improve the quality of fruits in his orchards to conducting experiments on peas. Knight was too early—he observed that some traits proved stronger than others, that some traits could re-appear after several generations of dormancy and that the progeny from crossbred peas were stronger than those from inbred peas—but the science wasn't yet mature enough to really understand the whys and wherefores behind his discoveries or to take it to the next step. It would take another 80 years before more experiments were conducted by Gregor Johann Mendel, a monk working in what is now the Czech Republic, before this science would advance.

Taking cuttings

Many shrubs, trees and some perennials can be grown from small lengths of stem or twig that are trimmed to size and encouraged to grow new roots. This is by far the easiest way to increase your stock of plants and, in some cases, the fastest way as well.

Take the cuttings just below a node and keep them fresh in a plastic bag until you plant them. Trim the leaves to reduce the amount of leaf area. Make soft cuttings about four to six inches long and woody cuttings about six to ten inches long. Dust the base of your cutting in a small amount of rooting powder and place them in a pot of very well drained compost, label it and cover with a plastic bag. Keep the cuttings in a shady spot until well rooted and keep the rooting medium moist but not wet.

All soft cuttings should be taken in spring or early summer while hardwood cuttings should be taken in the winter. Different plants respond to different methods.

Softwood and semi-ripe cuttings

Cut healthy stems from this years growth, trim them, place them around the edge of a pot and cover with a plastic bag. Good for lavender, rosemary, and many other woody herbs, pelargoniuns, berry fruits, *Ceanothus*, *Forsythia* and *Philadelphus*.

Hardwood cuttings

Remember to cut the top of a cutting at an angle (this sheds water and reminds you which way is up) and the bottom just below a node, which is where most of the growth hormones are. Good for most deciduous shrubs, including fruit bushes, most vines and climbers, and many trees.

Nodal cuttings with a heel

Take the cutting from a side shoot, where it joins the branch, and include a nick out of the branch with each cutting. Good for *Cotinus*, *Lonicera*, honeysuckle and jasmin.

Basal cuttings

These are the same as nodal cuttings, but taken right from the bottom of the plant, near soil level. Good for asters, chrysanthemum, delphinium, lupins, phlox and salvia.

Root cuttings

These are sunk horizontally in some soil mixed with sharp sand and left in a shady spot until shoots appear. Good for *Chaenomeles*, *Clerodendron* *Romneya coulteri*, sumac, acanthus, dicentra, echinacea, eryngium.

1
2
3
4

Dividing

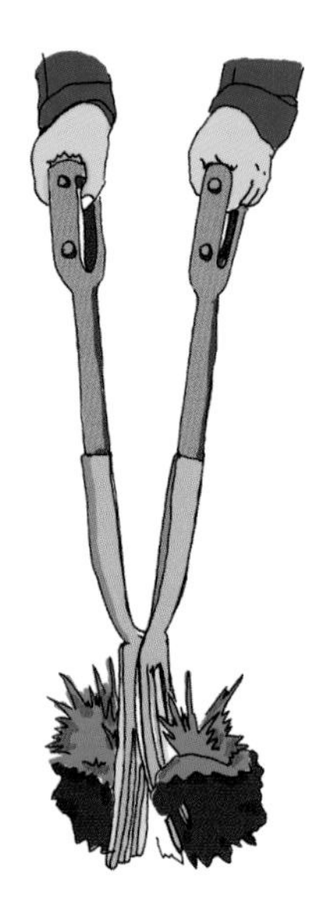

Most clump-forming plants, like daylilies, rhubarb and mint can be quickly propagated by division. Depending on the size of the mother plant, dig it up and divide it into smaller pieces. Solid roots such as rhubarb are sliced through with a sharp spade, ensuring each new clump has a healthy root and a healthy crown. Fibrous root clumps are levered apart by inserting two garden forks, back to back, into the middle of the root mass, lever the roots apart, soak in bucket of muddy water in the shade for 15 minutes and replant in their new home. Clumps of rhizomes such as Iris can be lifted and sections sliced off with a sharp garden knife.

As long as each section of root has an eye at the top for stem growth and a bit of root at the bottom, it will grow into a healthy new plant. Discard any part of the clump that shows sign of disease or rot, and replant at the original soil level. Many plants respond to division with renewed vigour.

Grafting

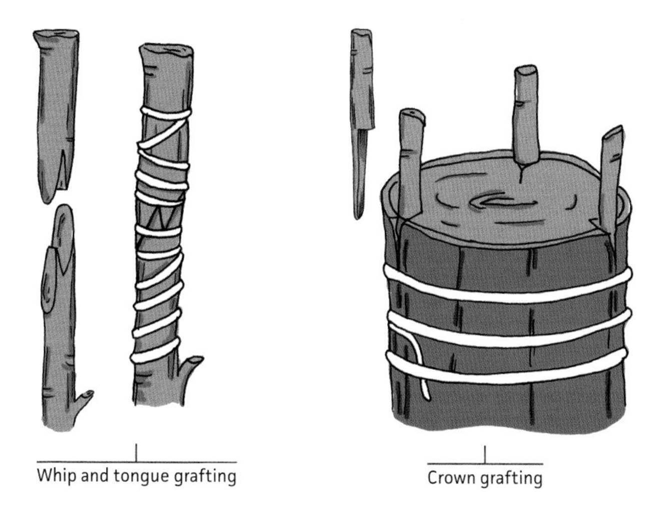

Grafting has been around for at least 4,000 years. There are several very different reasons for grafting one plant onto another. It can be a way of combining the fruiting or flowering features of the scion—the stem—with the growth habit (such as dwarfing habit) or resilience (such as disease or weather resistance) of the rootstock.

Old orchards can be rejuvenated quickly and comparatively cheaply by top working; grafting new varieties onto existing roots can bring the orchard back into production in a fraction of the time of replanting. Many conifers that don't root easily as cuttings, will graft effortlessly.

To successfully graft one plant onto another you must align the tissues in the scion with that of the rootstock.

The cuts must be very smooth and clean, with no messy edges that would rot or allow disease organisms to enter. Whatever type of graft is practiced, the cambium layer of the scion must be in contact with the cambium (the green layer just under the bark) of the rootstock as this will stimulate the growth of the cutting.

Layering

Layering is simply taking cuttings backwards. Instead of taking the cutting first and encouraging it to root, you first encourage it to root and then you remove it from the mother plant. Some plants will readily root whenever the growing tip comes in contact with soil, some where the nodes or joints touch the ground and some will root along the whole length of a stem. In each case hold the branch in place with a stone or a piece of bent wire.

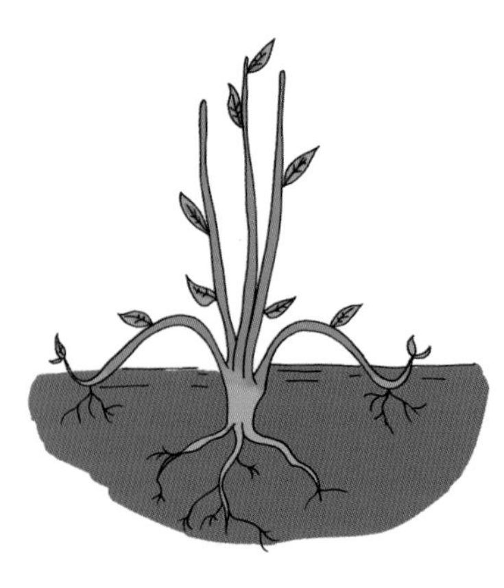

Simple layering

Simple layering is encouraging a root to grow at a node along the length of a flexible branch and is suitable for climbing roses, forsythia, rhododendron, honeysuckle, box and azaleas.

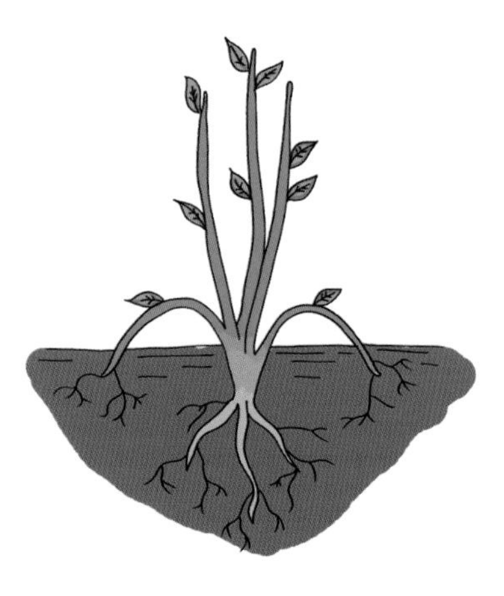

Tip layering

Tip layering encourages the tip of a branch to root. Good for purple and black raspberries, blackberries, Vinca major.

Compound layering

As its name suggests, is encouraging several nodes to develop roots along the same length of stem and is suitable for vine-like growth such as, wisteria, clematis, grapes, honeysuckle, hops, Parthenocissus species and climbing hydrangea.

Mound layering

Mound layering is achieved by mounding soil around the main stem or stems of the chosen plant. This method is suitable for spirea, quince, daphne, magnolia, cotoneaster, Cotinus and dogwoods.

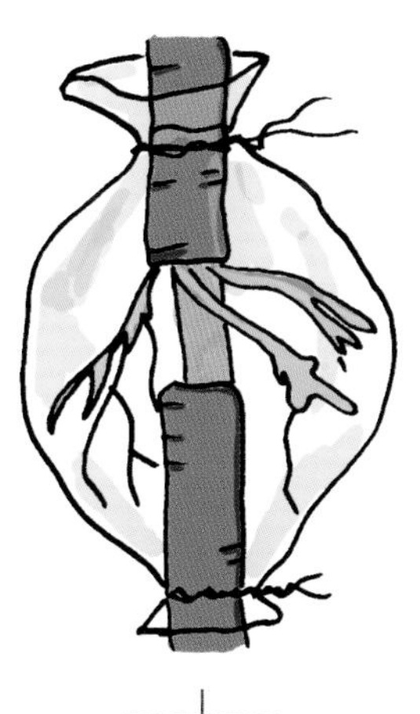

Air layering

Air layering is a means of encouraging above-ground stems to form roots. This is done by making a small cut in the stem, dusting the injury with rooting hormone and placing damp moss in the cut to hold it open. Pack more moss around the stem to keep it moist and enclose the area in a plastic bag until rooting takes place.

Apples & Rootstocks

For plant breeders apples are a bit of a pain. They are very promiscuous, cross-fertilising with all the trees in the neighbourhood, which results in each new seedling growing into a unique individual. While this is great as far as being able to grow lots of new and different varieties of apples, it isn't great if you like the variety that you already have and you want more of it. In order to propagate the same variety of fruit, apples need to be budded or grafted onto another rootstock, and which rootstock is chosen will determine the ultimate size, vigour and precocity (the age at which the tree will first bear fruit) of the tree as well as its ability to cope with certain diseases, climate conditions and soils. To get the best out of your apples you need to choose the correct rootstock. Most rootstocks that are used around the world today have been developed by the East Malling Research Station in England. New developments by Cornell University, known as the "G-series", have resulted in rootstocks that impart increased resistance to the disease fireblight, and increased cold tolerance necessary for apples grown in some areas of North America. The "B-series" is a Russian development, noted for its cold tolerance.

M27 is extremely dwarfing and good for pyramids or stepovers, in pots or around vegetable beds and freestanding in small gardens. It is possible to grow a whole orchard in a small garden if they are grown on M27.

M9 is used for similar purposes as M27 and early fruiting but requires a permanent stake

M26 & MM106 are good rootstocks for small to medium sized gardens growing three to four metres tall. MM106 is best avoided in cold areas.

G11 produces a tree of about the same size as M26 but better suited to North American conditions. Affords some resistance to fire blight, woolly aphid, and collar rot.

MM111 (vigorous) and M25 (very vigorous) are for standard trees only and are rather too large for most sites, but are ideal for growing as very large fans, or in community orchards.

G16 is a good alternative to M9 for areas of the USA where Fireblight is an issue. Other attributes are similar to M9.

B118 produces a tree of similar size to the popular MM111 rootstock, but with far better cold-hardiness.

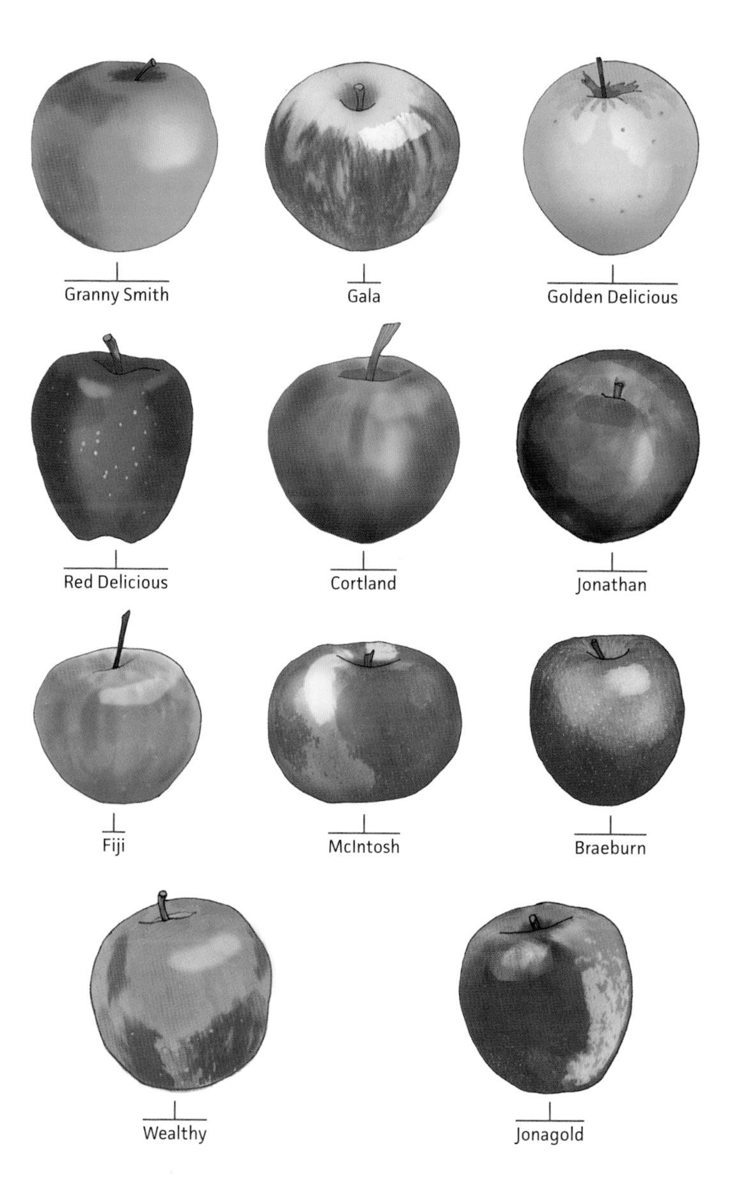
Granny Smith
Gala
Golden Delicious
Red Delicious
Cortland
Jonathan
Fiji
McIntosh
Braeburn
Wealthy
Jonagold

Tree Forms

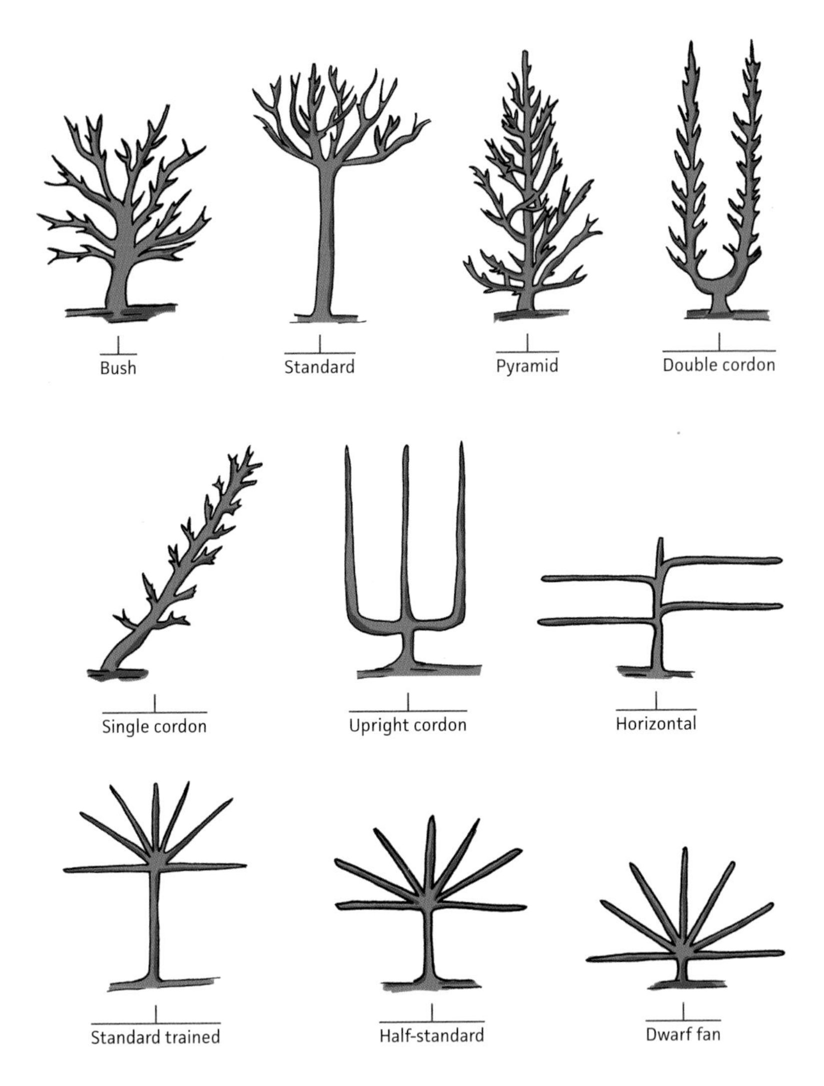

Bush
Standard
Pyramid
Double cordon
Single cordon
Upright cordon
Horizontal
Standard trained
Half-standard
Dwarf fan

Sports & Chimera

Sports or mutations are spontaneous changes in the appearance of any part of a plant. Some, like variegated leaves, twisted stems or double flowers, are often considered desirable. If the change in the cells that cause the mutation arise at the growing point, of a branch for instance, the whole branch may exhibit the effect and if the mutation proves stable, it can be used to propagate a whole new line of plants. However, if the mutation arises at the base of a single leaf or flower the effect will be fleeting.

In the case of variegation, if left unchecked the reversion will win out as the pure green leaves will always be able to outgrow the variegated ones, simply because they contain more chlorophyll… a frequent example of this is the variegated *Acer* 'Drummondii' which can often be seen with large areas of plain green leaves in the canopy of otherwise cream and green variegation. Mutations frequently appear as a result of a viral infection and will continue throughout the life of the plant, becoming so stable that they almost never revert, like the flowering maple *Abutilon*. The mosaic virus that causes the leaves of the *Abutilon* to appear mottled yellow doesn't appear to affect the health of the plant in any way.

Some chimeras will never come true from cuttings. The gold-edged Mother-in-law's-tongue, *Sansevieria trifasciata Laurentii*, will only produce green leaves from cuttings. This curious habit arises because the new plant only grows from the green part of the green/gold mother plant so only the green part can be replicated. If you want to propagate a plant with the same variegation as the mother *sansevieria*, you must do it by root division.

A very few chimeras are created by grafting so that the new plant is literally a confusion of the two plants from which it is created. The chimera + *Laburnocytisus* '*Adamii*' was created when grafting a laburnum, *Laburnum anagyroides*, and a broom, *Chamaecytisus purpureus* together. The plus sign before the genus indicates a graft chimera (as opposed to the x sign that precedes the genus names in a intergeneric hybrids). This strangely attractive plant is part laburnum and part cytisus, producing the leaf and flowers types of both parents. The genetic material is mixed without actually fusing as it would in a true hybrid, and under the microscope a cross-section of a stem looks like a mosaic made up of the separate cell tissues.

pH & Soil Testing

pH is the scale used to measure the acidity or alkalinity of soil. Seven is neutral. Anything under seven is acid and anything over seven is alkaline.

For practical purposes, most plants are happiest at the 'neutral' level of 6.5 to seven on the scale. This is because most plant nutrients are locked up (chemically speaking) at either end of the scale, while manganese and aluminium will be available in levels toxic to most plants. Soil microbes, bacteria and fungi all work best in the mid-range, and will die if conditions become too extreme. Most of us find ourselves on soils that are only slightly either side of seven.

If in doubt buy a soil test kit or if you are very clever take a close look at the weeds in your garden; sorrel, mullein, stinging nettle and wild pansy all thrive in acidic soils; salad burnet, scarlet pimpernel, nodding thistle, stinkweed and campion appreciate an alkaline soil.

Extremes of pH also alters the structure of the soil so, everything considered, the best way to alter soil pH and combat problems with nutrition and soil structure at the same time is to add organic matter which is loaded with beneficial beasties. Mix in composted oak or pine leaves or bark and spent mushroom compost to lower the pH or add wood ashes and ground limestone mixed with garden compost to raise the pH.

There is controversy about what the p in pH stands for, though there is general agreement that the H stands for hydrogen. The p is thought to mean either—percentage of hydrogen, potential of hydrogen or power of hydrogen. The point to remember is that a soil with of a pH of six contains ten times more hydrogen ions than a soil with a pH of seven, and a soil with a pH of five contains 100 times more than a soil with pH seven.

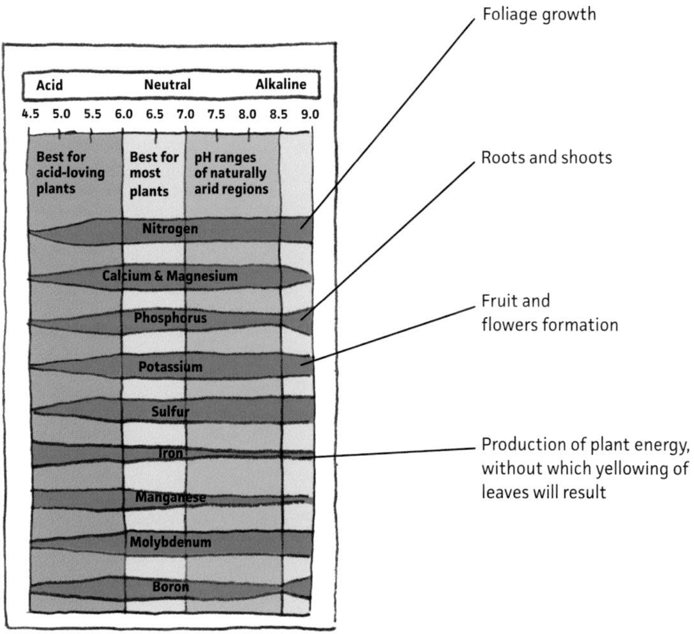

Acid Neutral Alkaline

4.5 5.0 5.5 6.0 6.5 7.0 7.5 8.0 8.5 9.0

Best for acid-loving plants

Best for most plants

pH ranges of naturally arid regions

Nitrogen

Calcium & Magnesium

Phosphorus

Potassium

Sulfur

Iron

Manganese

Molybdenum

Boron

Foliage growth

Roots and shoots

Fruit and flowers formation

Production of plant energy, without which yellowing of leaves will result

Plants for acid soils

Azalea, bayberry, blackberry, blueberry, butterfly weed, cardinal flower, chrysanthemum, cranberry, flax, heath, heather, huckleberry, lillies, lily of the valley, lupine, marigold, kalmia, oak peanut, pecan, potato, radish, raspberry, rhododendron, spruce, sweet potato, watermelon, yew.

Plants for alkaline soils

Allysum, asparagus, bean, beet, cabbage, cantaloupe, carnation, cauliflower, celery, cucumber, geum, iris, lettuce, mignonette, nasturtium onion, parsnip, pea, phlox, rhubarb, salsify, squash, sweet pea.

NPK & Plant Nutrition

NPK are letters found on the packets of fertilisers, always in the same order, and they simply mean N for nitrogen, P for phosphorus and K for potassium (also known as potash). These are, of course, the chemical symbols for the elements as found on the periodic table. They were once known as the three macronutrients but it is now known that plants require other nutrients in similarly large quantities and calcium (Ca), magnesium (Mg) and sulphur (S) have been added to the list of macronutrients.

There are a further seven micronutrients (or trace elements) that plants require in smaller quantities, but are still essential for healthy growth: boron (B), chlorine (Cl), copper (Cu), iron (Fe), manganese (Mn), molybdenum (Mo), and zinc (Zn). Certain plant diseases are caused by deficiencies in one or more of these nutrients and while careful detective work and much perusing of a good plant disease manual may lead you to the correct answer, it is probably quicker and definitely more accurate in the long run to send a soil sample off to the local agricultural extension service or horticultural society.

You can add most of the nutrients that your plants need by adding compost and other organic conditioners to your soil such as well rotted manure or composted bark supplemented with nettle or comfrey soup. Both nettles and comfrey are rich in phosphorus and potassium as well as several micronutrients. Make up the soup by filling a bucket half full of leaves, then topping it up with water. Cover the mix (it is very stinky) and leave it for two or three weeks, then use it as a fertiliser, diluted at a rate of ten parts water to one part soup. Nettle and comfrey soup also makes a great foliar feed to give a quick boost to your plants, just remember to avoid spraying it directly onto fruit or salad crops.

An old way of preparing the soup was to fill a sack full of nettles or comfrey leaves, tie up the end and suspend it in a water butt or rain barrel; the resulting liquid could then be used straight from the tap.

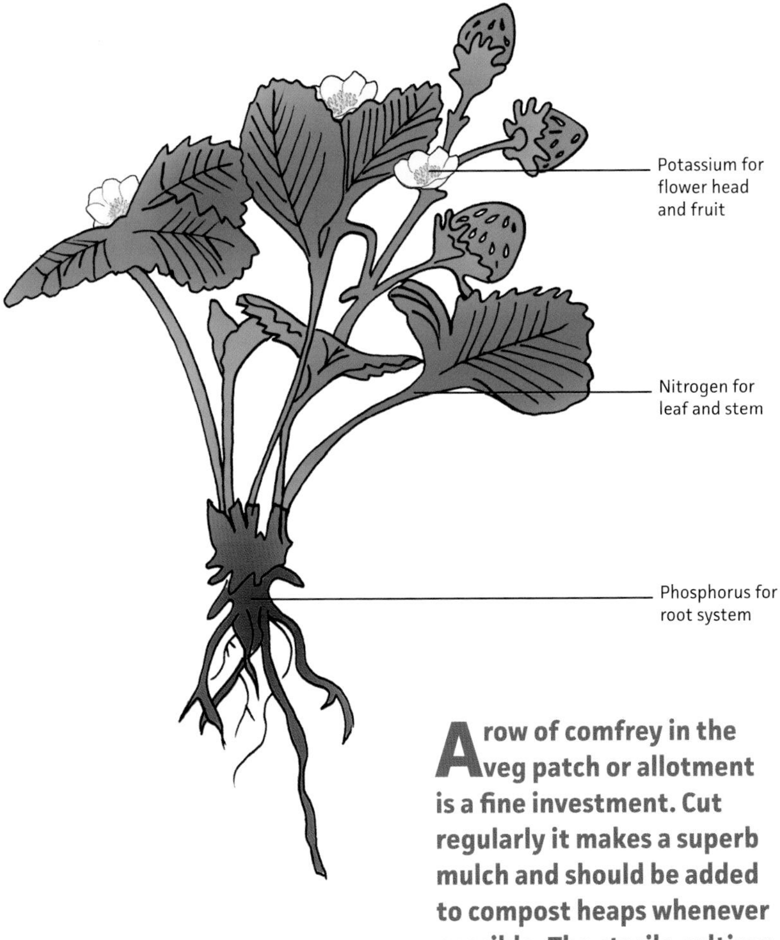

Potassium for
flower head
and fruit

Nitrogen for
leaf and stem

Phosphorus for
root system

A row of comfrey in the veg patch or allotment is a fine investment. Cut regularly it makes a superb mulch and should be added to compost heaps whenever possible. The sterile cultivar Blocking 14 wins all trials but regularly cut, any comfrey will pay dividends.

Composting

Nothing causes so much disappointment in the garden as the average compost heap. We are told time and again that all you need to do is to layer up all your old rubbish, give it a water now and then and turn it whenever you can and hey presto! a free and inexhaustible supply of lovely nutritious soil. Every word of that is true, but that does mean every word. You do need to layer it, water it occasionally and turn it. When the books say build your heap about four feet square, that is because that is the most efficient size for generating heat.

When they say cover the heap with a bit of old cardboard or carpet, that is because those materials allow some water and air ingress, but still protect the precious stuff from the odd deluge and keep it warm at the same time. It is possible—almost inevitable—that any heap of old kitchen and garden waste will rot down eventually. However whether it rots down slowly into a slimy mess or a hard, dry cake, or quickly into a delicious heap of fragrant soil, will depend on how you build it and how you look after it. You can add expensive compost activators that will start the rot, or you could simply add a layer of topsoil laden with soil microbes and mini-beasts every now and then, spiced up with some animal bedding whenever it is available. And one other thing—build your heap in a reasonably sunny spot—it will just sit and sulk in a cold dark corner. You can contain it in wood or plastic or wire, or simply leave it as a heap.

So... layer it, water it, turn it. Layer it, water it, turn it.

Properly made, you can have wonderfully rich compost in two months. There are ways—by shredding everything finely and turning the heap every couple of days—of making compost in two weeks in the warmth of summer; a good experiment, perhaps.

Worm Farming

A wormery or worm farm is another way of turning household and garden waste into soil and liquid feed for your garden, especially in small households with correspondingly small gardens where the amount of kitchen and garden waste is limited. A wormery can be purpose built or adapted from boxes or buckets, filled with layers of shredded and scrunched newspaper, waste and a clew (or some say, herd) of at least 100 brandling or tiger worms, ordered from a supplier or harvested from a mature compost heap.

Made properly, a wormery will quickly deal with any waste you care to throw at it. Add your fresh waste in small amounts, covered with a layer of lightly dampened newspaper, and ensure that the old waste has been processed by your worms before adding any more. Keep doing this until the bin is full of lovely rich and crumbly compost, then empty it and return the worms to the clean bin ready to start again. The worms will stay in the top layer so will be easy to collect and transfer.

The liquid that drains out of the worm compost must be used within 24 hours of harvesting; as it doesn't heat up in the way a good compost heap does, the liquid can be rich in pathogens. Used quickly and as a drench around roots, worm juice, as well as worm compost, is nutritious plant food.

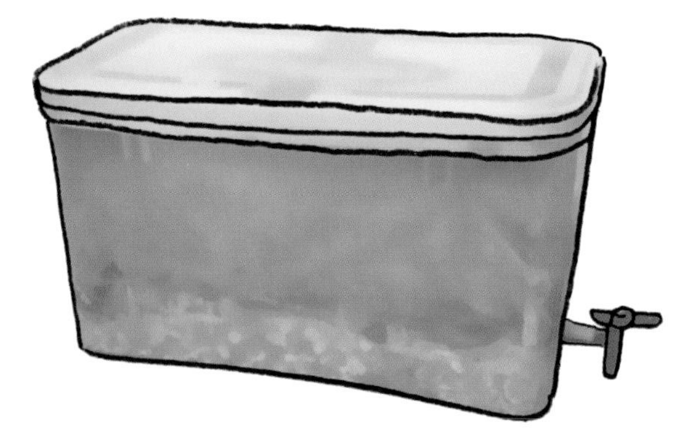

For Peat's Sake

Peat bogs are the result of many thousands of years of accumulation of partially decayed and compacted vegetation. As more and more plants are engulfed by the bog and the water table rises, the anaerobic environment becomes more acidic and prevents further decay.

There are many wonderful and fascinating things that are unique to peat bogs. At first glance a bog may appear to be a desolate place but a closer inspection reveals a world rich in highly specialised plants and animals (not to mention archaeological treasures) that are found nowhere else on earth. Bogs are home to several species of carnivorous plants that have developed into flesh eaters to compensate for the lack of nutrients on the stagnant land, as well as a whole community of acid loving mosses, lichens, shrubs and trees. An insect delighting in the name 'the hairy-canary fly' can live nowhere else, while other invertebrates, mammals, amphibians and reptiles use bogs as secure breeding sites.

Peat bogs are highly sensitive places that, if disturbed or removed, cannot simply be fixed or re-grown. Just as the vegetation is locked up within the bog, so is the carbon that it contains. If the bog is excavated or drained, the trapped carbon is unlocked and released into the atmosphere in colossal amounts as CO^2.

The destruction of peat bogs doesn't stop with the excavation of peat to add to a bag of compost. For each bag, there is the consequence of drainage and habitat destruction that reduces the excavation of peat to an act of criminal damage, compounded by the fact that there are very satisfactory alternatives available. When it comes down to it, sometimes it takes a bit of effort to ensure that gardening stays green.

Weeds

To quote a well-worn phrase, weeds are simply plants growing in the wrong place. In the hedgerow, wild clematis is a valuable winter food and bedding store for wildlife, while in the garden it is a rotten invader that constantly tries to swamp your cultivated clematis.

At the other end of the scale are those plants that are so invasive and so persistent that they strike terror into the hearts of anyone unfortunate enough to discover them. It is one good reason to always buy a house in the summer, so that you can see what you are inheriting in the garden. Japanese knot weed, Gout weed, creeping thistles, creeping buttercups and bindweed are all terrors of the border and veg patch.

If you are thinking of installing a rock garden think again unless you are very keen on hand weeding. The roots of any perennial weed, once established in the gaps between rocks, are a nightmare to remove. When it is impossible to remove the weed by pulling the whole thing out, the aim is to weaken it. Keep on removing the above ground portion and eventually it will weaken and the roots will die. Eventually.

Hoeing can be a pleasure, if you have the time and the weather. Get the weeds early, while they are still small and seedless and do it often and on sunny or windy days so that the severed plants dry out and die before they have a chance to root again. Collect up the debris, as many plants will continue to ripen seed for some time after they have been cut.

Hand weeding can be very therapeutic, if there isn't too much of it. Gloves can help, of course, but take the time to find some that really fit. For weeding in a garden that has a nettle invasion, there is no better device than a pair of rubber washing-up gloves.

Digging out weeds is often the only answer, especially if the roots of the weed have inveigled their way into a clump of one of your garden plants. Make yourself a cup of tea, dig out the whole lot and settle down for a session of unpicking.

Too many plants have earned themselves a less-than-honourable reputation simply by being so good at what they do—and what they do is multiply like mad in all sorts of ways. Digging over a veg patch or flower border that contains nettles, kudzu, bindweed or brambles will only result in a patch with even more of the same in a very short while. Each minute piece of root that is left in the soil will very rapidly develop into a whole new plant. For really persistent perennial weeds, such as Japanese knotweed, chemical weed killers may—rarely—be necessary but use them wisely and at the right time of year. Heed the warnings on the label. I am constantly surprised to see people spraying away happily clad in nothing more than a pair of shorts and top. Wear protective clothing and never, ever spray or dust anything on a breezy day.

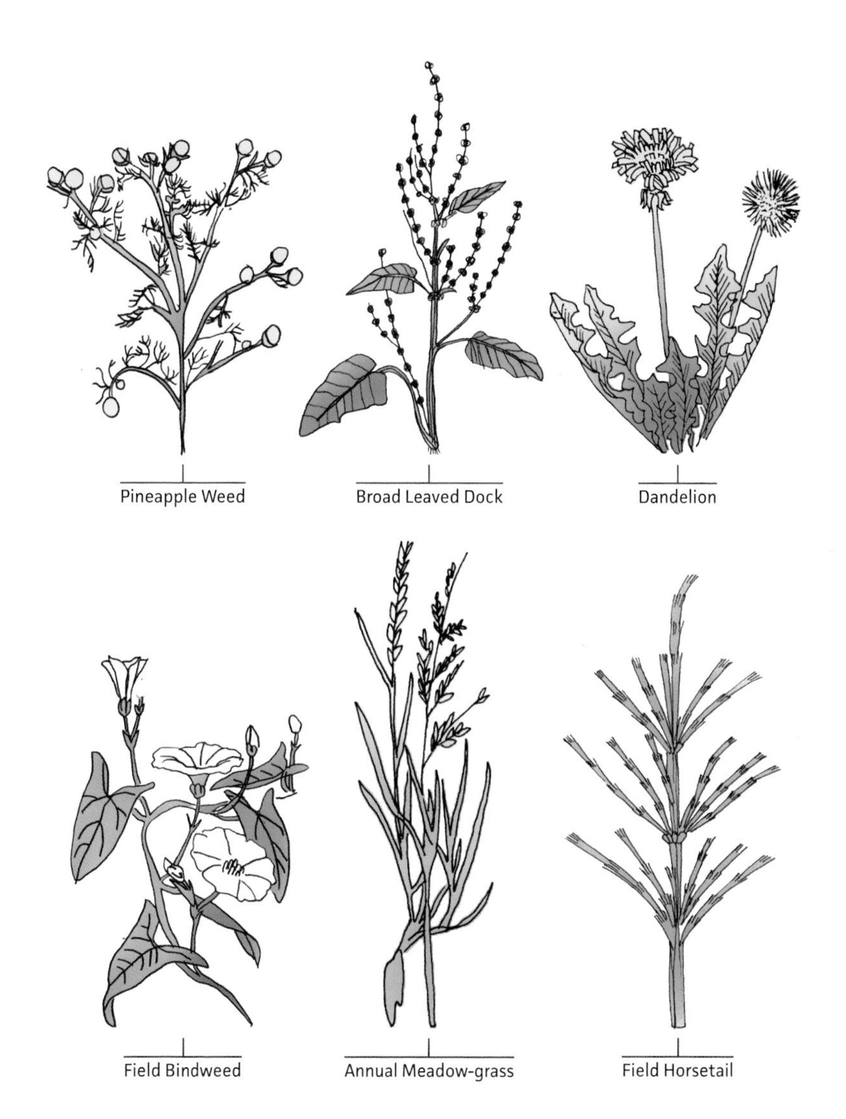
Pineapple Weed
Broad Leaved Dock
Dandelion
Field Bindweed
Annual Meadow-grass
Field Horsetail

Always weaken the weeds first. Begin by cutting the whole lot down, burning the debris and covering the area with heavy black plastic to omit light and moisture. For really persistent weeds, this on its own may not be enough. After several weeks, but still in the growing season, apply an approved weed killer and allow it to work. Sadly you may have to repeat this several times if the invasion is well established.

For plants that are inexorably entangled amongst the roots of an immovable neighbour the only other thing to try, if patience and time will allow, is to paint or spray the chemical on to the individual leaves of the pest and then enclose them in a bag or lay them out on the ground to let the chemical work its wickedness. Again, this may need to be repeated several times.

Mulches are an invaluable tool in the garden, especially as weed suppressors, but they are also invaluable in helping us to conserve water. Black plastic has its uses, but it is aesthetically unappealing and doesn't allow water to penetrate. Purpose made weed suppressors are expensive, have a limited life span and are variable in their effectiveness. Old natural fibre, hessian backed carpets are excellent if you can get them, especially on the allotment or the vegetable patch. For decorative purposes old leaves, pine needles, coco shells or chipped bark are the best and they do a terrific job. But be aware—alien fungi imported with bark mulch from Australia has become one of the latest unwanted foreign invaders to our gardens; use locally sourced bark if you possibly can.

Pouring boiling water on persistent individual weeds will kill them more quickly than any chemical, and a blast from a weed torch will do wonders!

Thistle
Creeping Buttercup
Shepherd's Purse
Common Chickweed
Nettle
Common Ragwort

Lawns

In the sixteenth century lawns developed as a fashion statement to demonstrate how well off and well-bred you were, a little bit like powdered wigs. Back then, in mild, moist Europe, the lawn was maintained by an army of manicurists, or by a flock of sheep. When the lawn moved across the ocean and into the suburbs, it retained its status-level—the bigger, broader and more visible, the better—but the sympathetic climate and the maintenance army had disappeared. No wonder the modern lawn is so time, money and ecologically expensive.

A great eco-friendly lawn is possible. The real key is to change the grasses you grow to those that are more suitable for your area, rather than the one that the chemical companies want you to grow so that they can sell you more chemicals. This will immediately free you from the feed-water-mow cycle. Incorporate other species in your lawn like nitrogen-fixing clovers—which, historically, have always been an 'acceptable' lawn plant. Feed only once a year, in the autumn, with a slow-release organic fertiliser, and dig out, rather than spray, any really unacceptable weeds. And finally, always, always raise the level of your mower to its maximum height to allow the grasses and other lawn plants to reach a height that will shade their roots and crowd out weeds.

Allowing a few invaders—daisies, violets, clovers—to nestle in among the grasses of your lawn can only be regarded as a good thing, both for wildlife and the health of the existing grass. (Think of all that frantic exchange going on between the plant roots and the fungal hyphae.) If you use chemicals on your lawn in the form of fertilisers or weed-killers, you, or your pets will be tracking them into the house every time you walk through the door. So break the cycle and go walking, sitting and playing on the grass, rather than just looking at it.

Lawn worship;
a strange religion.

Choosing grasses and other plants that are native to your area is the real key to growing a beautiful lawn, and looking for species that tolerate harsh conditions such as drought or heavy shade will make your lawn easy and inexpensive to look after. Aim for incorporating at least five different species of grasses and other plants in your seed mix for a healthy and vigorous lawn.

The no-rake way to caring for your lawn. The best way to deal with grass clippings is to leave them where they lie. Clippings contain 80 per cent water and a generous amount of nitrogen, exactly what you would put back on your lawn if you signed up to the expensive high maintenance programmes advocated by wealthy lawn maintenance companies. Instead, cut your grass regularly so the clippings are small and leave them to form a protective mulch on the soil which will further reduce the need for water, and will shade and shield the soil from invading weed seeds as well.

Slugs & Snails

Gardeners don't like slugs and snails. While some relish the battle of gardener vs. mollusc, venturing out in the dead of night armed with a torch and a pointy stick, others, particularly those of us who grow lettuce and hostas, can be driven to distraction when a previously pristine patch of succulent leaves has, overnight, been reduced to skeletal scraps by an unseen army of slimy molluscs. However it has to be said that the battle, if not the war, can be won; but not without understanding the enemy or protecting your loved ones.

With slugs, the first thing to grasp is that they are not all created equal. Bigger isn't necessarily meaner. The tiny, pale field slug, *Derocereas reticulatum*, that snuggles down inside a head of lettuce and devours it from within, is far more destructive than the more noticeable giant black slug with the orange fringe, *Arion ater*, who, surprisingly, prefers to munch his way through dead material.

Without the hindrance of a having to haul a house around slugs move much faster than snails, but they are also more vulnerable to the vagrancies of climate as they have no protection from drying out; you can use this to your advantage if you clear away all the places that slugs can hide. Once this is done lay out squares of cardboard or carpet in strategic places... these will act as great shelters for many sorts of creatures, from the beneficial beetles and bugs that patrol your garden to the real targets, slugs and snails looking for a cool damp place to lay up during the day. Beer traps have been proven to attract the slugs in droves, so share a bottle with the blighters once a week. Greenhouses, potting sheds and anywhere else where seedlings are housed can be particularly vulnerable.

Copper tape, which is supposed to deliver an electric shock, is a hit and miss affair, and rather expensive, so stick to the tried and tested methods. Try to install barriers to protect precious plants rather

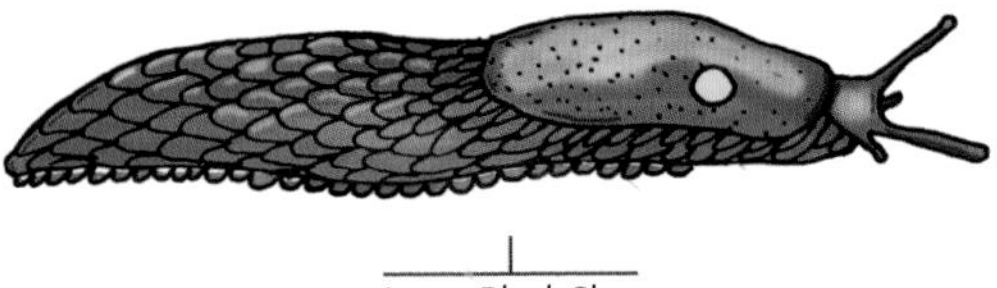

Large Black Slug

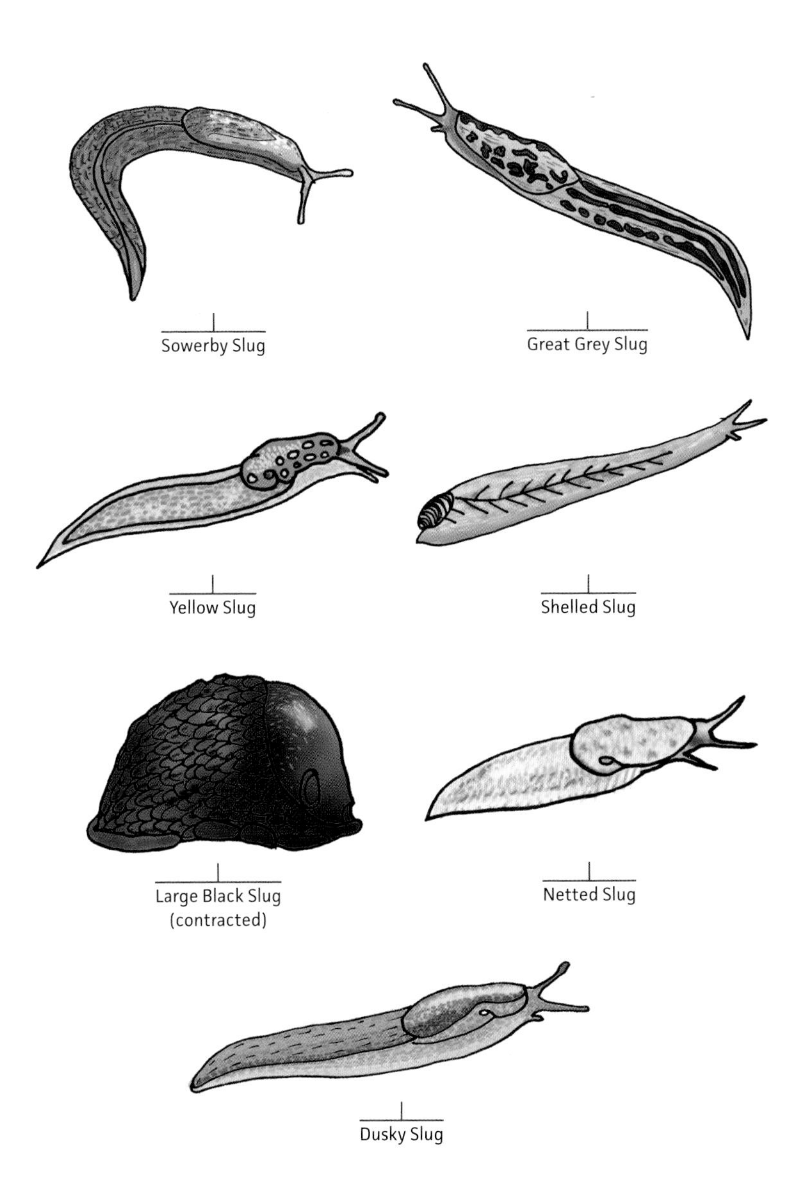
Sowerby Slug
Great Grey Slug
Yellow Slug
Shelled Slug
Large Black Slug
(contracted)
Netted Slug
Dusky Slug

Garden Snail
Strawberry Snail
Pellucid Glass Snail
Smooth Glass Snail
Round Mouthed Snail
White-lipped Snail

than always resorting to slug pellets (which are poisonous, even if they are listed as organic). Gravel, sharp sand, crushed eggshells, ashes or any other sharp or drying material will slow or stop the invaders.

If all else fails, nurture an interest in slugs and snails; they are fascinating little creatures. Both kinds are hermaphrodites, containing both male and female sexual organs. On a romantic encounter, two snails will sidle up alongside each other, nuzzling and entwining their heads. In many species each partner will attempt to fire a 'love dart', a calcium needle, into the other snail, just behind its head. This has the apparent benefit for the successful shooter, of making their sperm more appealing than that of any other potential suitor. Once each snail has fired its darts, and regardless if they have hit home (which they usually don't, snails being snails) copulation can then continue. As you would expect with these slow-motion creatures, mating can take a long time—several hours sometimes. The result, depending on the species, is either a clutch of eggs laid in a damp place or the live birth of dozens of tiny snails.

Slugs are, on the whole, more inventive with their mating techniques. Some indulge in elaborate chasing rituals where one slug leads the way, wagging its tail seductively while the other follows its slime trail. Others approach each other, stroking and licking and then adopt a yin yang position for mating. Once seen, the courtship of leopard slugs is never forgotten. After deciding that they are meant for each other the two slugs climb to a height and then suspend themselves from an iridescent slime rope and entwine themselves around each other before copulating in a rather spectacular and, it has to be said, beautiful manner.

Slug and snail free gardening

Clear up debris, old pots and anything else that provides a refuge; lay barriers and traps around vulnerable veg and precious plants. Collect slugs and snails each morning (feed them to chickens, put them out on the bird table or add them to your compost heap). In small areas try using nematodes—those microscopic organisms that love slugs and snails as much as you hate them—to control slug populations. These won't wipe out all slugs, but will help to limit numbers. Nematodes are available to order from garden centres or on line. Look out for slug and snail eggs laid in damp hollows, under stones and pots and in leaf litter. They look like a clump of fish eggs and can be opaque or transparent, depending on how mature they are.

Tools

There are those who garden with the bare minimum in the way of tools, and those that need a gadget to suit every purpose. If you belong to the latter group, you would have been quite at home during the great rise of interest in gardening in Britain when there truly was a tool for every task, right down to caterpillar shears, specifically designed to lop off any branches that harboured a web of caterpillars. For those in the first group you probably already have everything you need. Nevertheless a quick overview of tools is quite a pleasure, as a good tool makes every job easier and more enjoyable.

Spades are made for digging through all type of soil, so they must be strong, both in blade and handle. Buy a spade that suits you both in size and weight and be prepared to replace the handle every now and then. A good spade, like all garden tools, should last as long as you do. But, like the old joke about the broom that lasted for 20 years (it only had 17 new heads and 14 new handles), you may need to do some repairs now and then. Wooden handles—ash is best—are better than metal; the latter look strong, but up against heavy clay or stony ground the handle will lose every time. Unlike the broom head, the spade blade should endure.

Garden forks are used to break up heavy ground, to dig in stony ground—the tines ease their way between the stones more easily than the blade of a spade—and for disturbing the top layer of soil ready for raking and planting and for one of the most important jobs in the garden: turning the compost heap. If you want to make this job difficult, use a spade or shovel, otherwise use a fork. Again, size of head and handle are key to make the job comfortable.

Good secateurs are a pleasure to use. Anvil types must be exceptionally sharp or they will crush the stem, rather than cutting it cleanly. Scissor types are better for most jobs and a good pair, sharpened occasionally, will last a lifetime... if you don't lose them, which brings us to the last item.

Loppers, like large, long handled secateurs, are a must for easy pruning of large shrubs and trees, and those with extendable handles more than earn their extra cost in the time they save you not having to fetch a step ladder for minor tasks.

Synthetic garden chemicals are overrated and overused; much can be achieved by using a jet of water (or syringing, as the old books say), good nutrition and some herbal remedies such as a tea made from garlic to get rid of persistent pests.

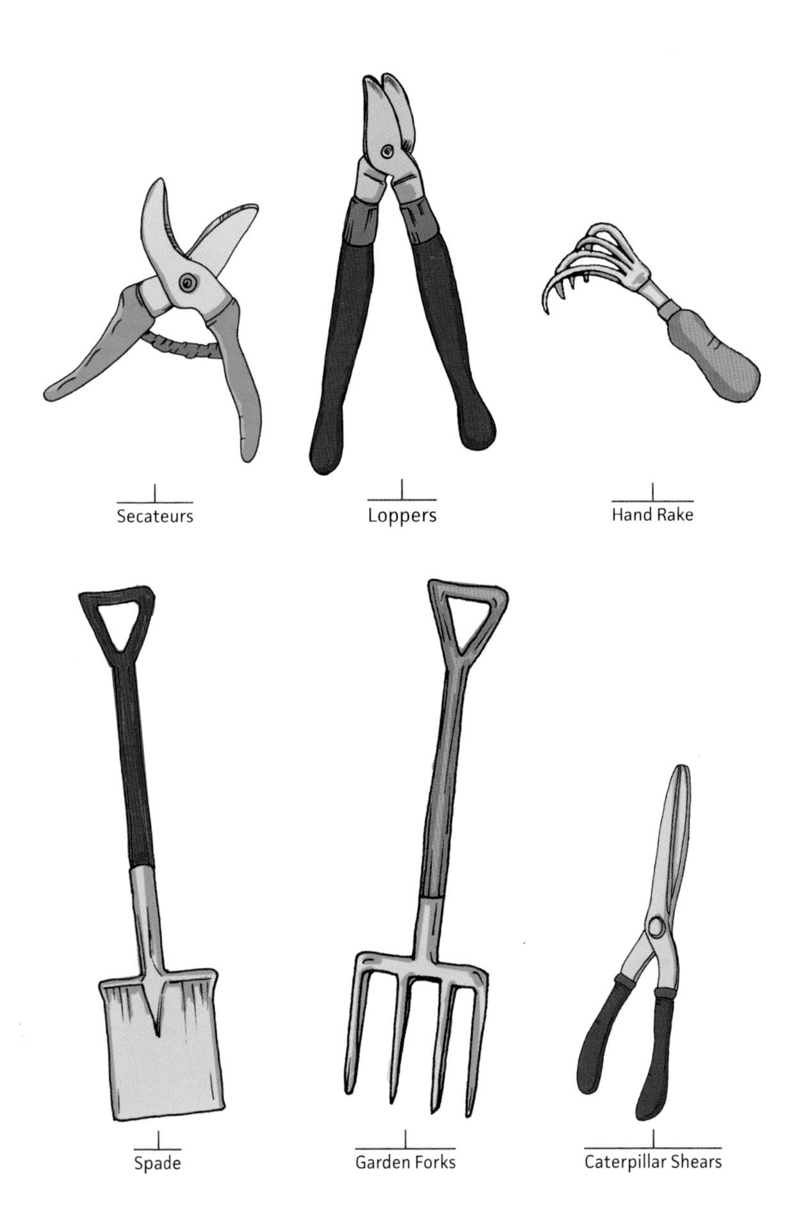
Secateurs
Loppers
Hand Rake
Spade
Garden Forks
Caterpillar Shears

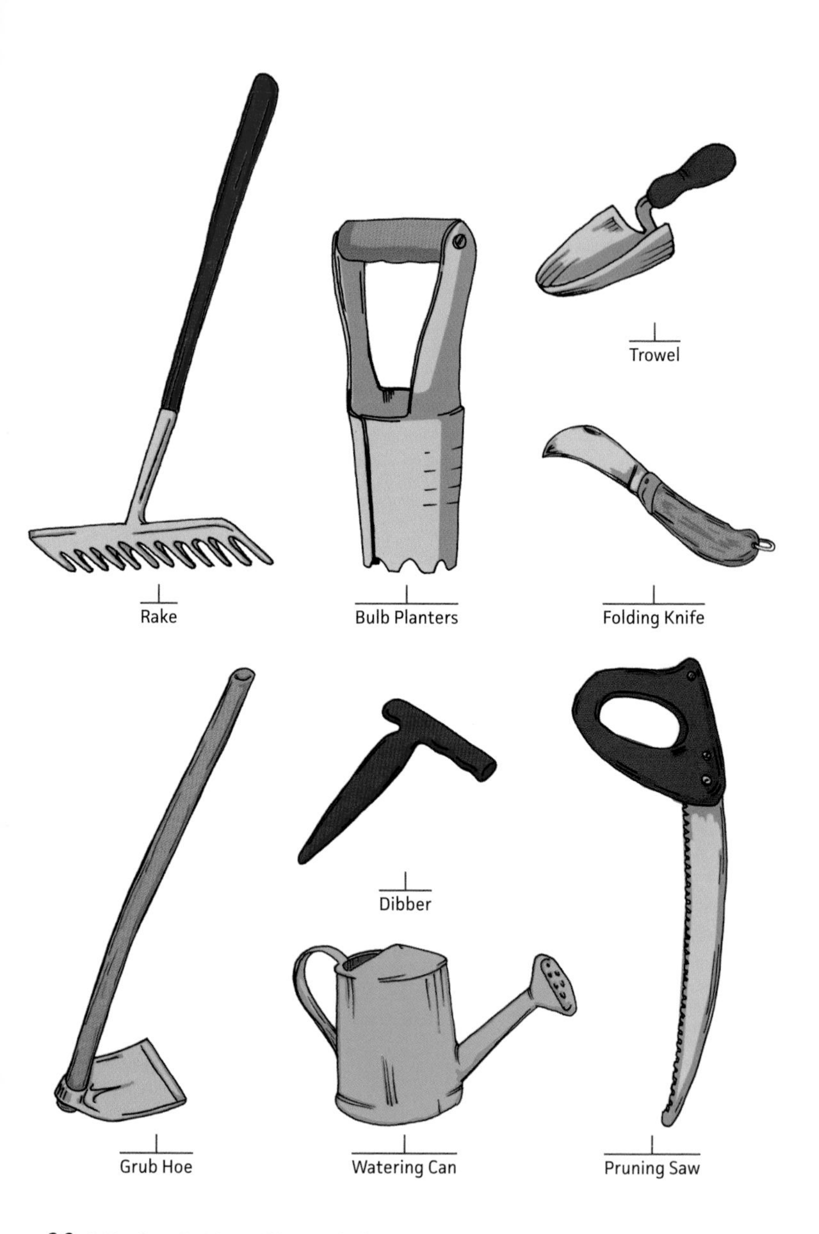
Trowel
Rake
Bulb Planters
Folding Knife
Dibber
Grub Hoe
Watering Can
Pruning Saw

Simply putting something in the way of the pests will usually do the trick. Barriers, either in the form of garden netting, cloches and mats made of cardboard, will stop the beasts from devouring your crops.

A very sharp, folding knife is invaluable in the garden. Used for cutting canes, budding, pruning and snipping string, such a knife, suspended from a rope and attached by a dog clip to a belt loop, will be used over and over.

Whoever set the trend for colouring the handles of garden implements brown or green has obviously never put a trowel down for a moment while they run to answer the phone, only to find it swallowed by the shrubbery, lost until the bareness of the winter garden reveals them again. The last essential item in the tool kit is a tin of florescent paint; colour the tool handles a vivid orange and you are at least giving yourself a chance—but whisper an apology to William Morris, who, upon visiting the Great Exhibition of 1851, refused to enter the Crystal Palace because the modern mass-market industrialism offended him. It offends me too, but I still want to find my trowel.

Depending on the nature and size of the garden, a folding pruning saw (kept oiled and out of the weather), a pick axe, a grub hoe (like a heavy-duty draw hoe with the blade set at 90 degrees to the handle), bulb planters, dibbers and dozens of more or less useful items will probably wheedle their way into the potting shed or tool store and many will rarely be used.

There are some neighbourhoods that join forces to share some of the useful but not-often-used garden tools. A lawn de-thatcher (a sharp-tined rake that removes the thatch of dead leaves around the roots of grasses) isn't often needed but neither is it easily substituted when it is required. Lawn edgers, as well as larger pieces of equipment such as rotovators, cultivators and shredders are all candidates for a simple use-and-return arrangement among neighbours or garden club members.

Garden Wildlife

Garden Wildlife

The most important thing a gardener can do for wildlife, after turning his back on chemicals, is to be a little messy. You don't have turn your garden into a wilderness, just don't be so quick to tidy up the signs of the passing seasons; a patch of grass allowed to grow long, standing hollow canes, seed heads left where they grow and the odd pile of brush wood are all superb steps towards making a wildlife friendly garden. Add to the mix a few well-stocked bird feeders and a hibernation hut or two and you have just about done it. The only other thing to consider is what plants you should grow. When choosing plants with wildlife in mind try to think of the community that you may be introducing into your garden.

Native plants already have a whole food web established with themselves at the heart, while introduced species support a vastly reduced community. Oaks, which invaded Britain after the retreat of the last ice age around 7,000 years ago, are home to more than 280 species of invertebrates. Sycamores (*Acer pseudoplatanus*) which were introduced a meagre 500 years ago only support about ten species. The general rule for wild gardening is to incorporate as many native plants into your garden as you can, not for the sake of the plants themselves, but in order to encourage the community they sustain.

Highly hybridised flowers, as a by-product of being continually selected for colour, size, flower form or disease resistance have often, accidentally, had their pollen- and nectar-bearing ability bred out of them so these will obviously be no good for supporting bees, hoverflies, butterflies or any other pollinating insect. By all means grow Pelargoniums, Begonias and Busy Lizzies, but make sure you grow nectar-rich plants as well.

There are hundreds of species of moth and butterfly, many of which rarely breed in gardens, preferring instead to lay their eggs on meadow plants, under the bark of native tree species or near ant's nests of one type or another. However butterflies and moths are fascinating and valuable members of the garden community and beneficial to our plants.

Amphibians and reptiles are keen garden dwellers, most often seen around old walls, woodpiles and ponds, and are valuable predators of garden pests as well as fascinating creatures in their own rights. Some frogs and toads become very blasé about the human traffic in their gardens, staying put and tolerating quite close contact if they believe that you are harmless.

Hazards in the garden include all sorts of seemingly innocuous items, as well as the poisons that are obviously better avoided.

Garden netting and discarded twine can be a death trap to small mammals, amphibians and reptiles. Bottles, tin cans with the lids not fully removed and uncovered rain barrels cause terrible distress to visiting creatures.

If you already grow fruit trees and bushes, vegetables or any other plant that needs pollination in order to do its job —such as producing attractive winter berries—then attracting—as many pollinating insects—into your garden as you can just makes sense.

Wildlife Friendly Pest Control

Poisons, be they bug sprays or slug pellets, don't only affect the target species as you might expect. Even the highly sophisticated chemicals that are now available can cause an imbalance by reducing the numbers of certain species upon which other, beneficial species depend. When you knock out the pest population on a particular plant, the creatures that preyed upon them will either move elsewhere or be knocked out themselves. Pest species, aphids for example, tend to breed more quickly than their predators, so after a while the pests will return in force while the predator population lags behind, leaving your plants even more vulnerable than before. It is always better to try and encourage the predators rather than wipe out the pests, as it will be less trouble and expense in the long run.

Build up a good community of ladybirds, lacewings, hoverflies and various predatory beetles by planting a range of nectar rich flowers—many predators are nectiverous when they are adult, but fiercely predatory in their larval stage—and provide areas that can act as nurseries for beneficial insects. Include lots of aromatic herbs, clump forming grasses and real bug magnets like sunflowers, cornflowers and local wildflowers. Choosing local flowers means that you aren't trying to educate your beneficial insects about new plants.

Encourage larger predators, like birds, frogs, toads, lizards, snakes and small mammals like hedgehogs, shrews and bats to make your garden the number one stop on the foraging trail by providing hideaways and feeding stations.

Furnish yourself with a couple of excellent guides to the wild species that inhabit your region, along with a powerful magnifying glass and a reasonable pair of binoculars and sit back occasionally just to enjoy the show.

Birds in the Garden

Birds are at the very heart of a wildlife garden and they are some of the easiest creatures to invite in and to tempt back. Provide a well-stocked feeding station all through the year and a good, safe supply of water and you need do little else. However, if you also provide a good range of plants that produce seeds and berries, and put up nest boxes, you will be increasing your enjoyment enormously as you will be privy to a whole range of behaviours that you would otherwise miss.

Site your various feeders, boxes and baths in a clear area with shrubs or other hiding places no closer than six feet (two metres) away so cats can't sneak up on your guests, and make use of the various pigeon and squirrel-proof feeders that are available to ensure that your feeders aren't emptied before the real target species have had their fill.

An inexpensive pair of binoculars (an expensive pair will be too powerful for the average garden) and a good field guide are essential for your full enjoyment of the bird life in your garden. You don't need to know anything about birds in order to enjoy them, nor do you have to feel the need to adopt an anorak and binoculars as your everyday dress code. However it does lend an extra depth if you know a little something about some of them. If you know that the swallows swooping over your garden are just stocking up on their way to a winter holiday in Africa or South America, and that 200 years ago the knowledgeable men of science still believed that when the swallows disappeared over winter they were hibernating in the bottom of lakes, you can feel as if you have been formally introduced.

Visiting birds, even seed eaters, need bugs and grubs to feed to their young in the spring. Birds need somewhere to nest, somewhere to rest and year round food and water. In the winter an extra meal of some fatty foods such as mealworms and suet balls will sustain your garden visitors through the cold.

Bees & Hoverflies

Pollination is as essential for us as it is for the individual flowers and there are some creatures, namely bees, that take on more than their fair share of pollination duties. Honey bees have been in the news because of various threats to their existence, with the upsurge in infestations by the deadly *veroa* mite and the devastating increase in incidence of colony collapse disorder. (Moving thousands of hives vast distances across continents in order to pollinate orchards for fruit and nut production virtually guarantees the weakening of the community and the spread of disease.) The threat to honey bee populations, coupled with the decline in bumble bee and solitary bee populations due to a loss of habitat means that there is a very real threat to our ability to grow a huge number of crops for our own consumption, never mind considering the survival of individual bee species.

New research suggests that today one of the most important sources of nectar and pollen for bees are gardens. With the catastrophic decline in mixed meadows and permanent pasture (which traditionally contained plants like clovers) and the resultant loss in nectar-rich flowers, gardens have become vitally important.

Bumble bees, in particular, are masters of their craft, as there are several flowers that cannot be fertilised in any other way. This is because bumble bees grasp the anther and vibrate their wing muscles at speeds of up to 200 miles an hour which releases the pollen, just like the salt being shaken out of a salt cellar. No other pollinating insect does this and it means that, if bumble bees face a decline so do, inevitably, several species of plants. Bees are often employed in vast commercial greenhouses as tomato pollinators, clocking in to do a day's work in exchange for a feast of sweet, tomato nectar. They have the additional advantage over the honey bee in that they will continue to work in cool and rainy weather, which honey bees are unable to do.

Bumble bees produce no honey as they do not overwinter in hives and therefore they don't need to store food supplies to maintain the colony, as do honey bees. Only the queen bumble bee overwinters, tucking herself under a pile of dry leaves or grasses or holing up in an old mouse nest.

You may see a queen foraging for nectar on warm days in winter, so a few winter flowering shrubs and perennials would be beneficial, but generally she will stay tucked up until the weather warms again in spring. Then she will find herself a warm, dry hole at the base of a wall or in a sunny bank and she will begin to lay eggs, all the while taking trips out to gather nectar and pollen to feed herself and, later, her babies. She fashions a small pot out of wax, and fills it with honey to sustain her if the weather is poor. Just like a hen, she has a small hairless patch on her abdomen which allows her body heat to warm her

Bilberry Bumblebee
Bombus monticola

Garden Bumblebee
Bombus hortorum

Buff-tailed Bumblebee
Bombus terrestris

Red-tailed Bumblebee
Bombus lapidarus

Early Bumblebee
Bombus pratorum
Common Carder Bee
Bombus pascuorum
White-tailed Bumblebee
Bombus lucorum
Brown-banded Carder Bee
Bombus humilis
Barbut's Cuckoo Bee
Bombus barbutellus

eggs as she sits on them. All the time she is nesting she must make quick trips out to the immediate neighbourhood to visit flowers to collect nectar and honey. If she is gone for too long her eggs will cool down and die. Having a good supply of nutritious flowers close by is imperative.

Many solitary bees are valuable pollinators, who repay a little close inspection. One of the most charming are the leaf-cutter bees that may advertise their presence by the little semi-circular holes that they cut from the edge of rose leaves. If you spot the signs it is a treat to follow the flight back to the nesting site—a hole in soft wood, a tunnel in an earth bank or the pithy stems of roses or brambles—where the bee will roll the leaf into a tube and tuck it, along with a supply of nectar and pollen, into the little tunnel and lay an egg. Then off she will go again, to collect a fresh lot of supplies.

The blue mason bee, which mines out little nest tunnels in mortar, the hairy-footed flower bee, which approaches its flower target with its tongue already extended and at the ready, the orchard bee which is employed by farmers to pollinate fruit trees, the carpenter bee and the wool carder bee which scrapes the hairs off leaves to line her nests, just like a woman carding wool, these are just some of the charming little bees that work tirelessly around the flowers of your yard and garden.

Many fly species, but most particularly hoverflies, are champion pollinators. Hoverflies, those great mimics of wasps and bees, often have fascinating life-cycles. Several live in the sap runs of trees, (what a specialised environment!) while others have an aquatic stage, with one in particular (the unfortunately named rat-tailed maggot) being able to breath underwater by means of a snorkel that it grows from its tail end. About one third of all species of hoverflies are aphid predators in their larval stage which makes them indispensible members of the beneficial insect brigade. Hoverflies are much overlooked as valuable garden members and are habitually mistaken for the wasps and bees that they often impersonate. True to their name, hoverflies can easily be identified by their practice of darting around and hanging in mid-air, but a closer look can also tell you if you are looking at a male or a female; the males eyes always meet in the middle, while a female's eyes have a gap between them.

Ponds

If you were to do only one thing in your garden to actively encourage wildlife, the thing to do would be to make a pond, even a small one. This habitat will provide breeding and feeding opportunities for frogs, toads, newts and countless invertebrates. Mammals and birds will visit to hunt and to drink.

If possible the pond should be dug into the ground but if that doesn't work for you, then even a large bucket of water left in the semi-shade will encourage more wildlife than you can imagine. A slightly raised pond with a seating platform around one side will provide hours of enjoyment and the addition of a heavy duty grill will allay any fears about pond safety.

Surround your pond with plenty of sheltering plants so that the frogs, newts and toads will have somewhere to hole up in the heat of the day, and always supply a ramp so that if an animal should fall in, it can easily find its way back to dry land.

The simplest garden pond is a hole dug in a corner of the garden and lined with heavy duty plastic. Dig the hole at least one and a half feet (45cm) deep, and line the bottom with old carpet, sand or something similar to prevent stones from puncturing the plastic. Lay the lining up and over the edge and fill your pond with water before trimming the plastic. Cover the edges with turf or stone to stop the lining from flopping over into the water. Now the fun bit, as you add water plants, the ramp and the marginal plants and watch the wildlife flood in.

Always provide hideaways for amphibians and reptiles around the pond margins so that they have somewhere safe to hide in during the day. A broken terracotta pot half sunk in the soil, and loosely furnished with straw will make a weather resistant home for these useful creatures.

In hot seasons resist the desire to top up the pond with tap water as it can cause an imbalance in the chemistry of the pond. Use rain water instead, and then only when really necessary.

Plants for Wildlife

Winter berries

- holly
- mahonia
- pyracantha
- cotoneaster
- viburnum tinus
- dog rose
- hawthorn
- mountain ash
- ivy
- berberis

Seed plants

- teasel
- dandelion
- thistles sunflowers
- goldenrod
- evening primrose
- ornamental grasses
- clematis
- Michaelmas daisy
- rosa rugosa

Meadow flowers

- annual cornflower
- oxeye daisy
- cowslips
- ragged robin
- red campion
- harebell
- wild marjoram
- chicory
- vipers bugloss
- clover

Ten herbs to attract bees, butterflies, hoverflies and lacewings

- lavender
- parsley
- marjoram
- rosemary
- chives
- pot marigolds
- fennel
- dill
- borage
- sage

Bee plants

try to plant a selection that will provide a meal all the year round...

Spring	*Summer*
fruit tree blossoms	vipers bugloss
lungwort	white and red clover
primroses	honeysuckle
cranesbills	stachys lanata
	foxgloves
	purple toadflax

Nectar plants

- honeysuckle
- bistort
- verbena bonariensis
- buddleia
- sedum
- marigolds
- geraniums
- yarrow
- fennel
- calendula

Multi-purpose plants

- buddleia
- elder
- crabapple
- ivy
- rosa rugosa
- lavender
- marjoram
- sunflowers
- plum trees
- honeysuckle

Night-scented plants to encourage moths and bats

- evening primrose
- flowering tobacco
- night scented stocks
- honeysuckle
- white jasmine
- red valerian
- single pinks
- soapwort
- campions
- hemp agrimony

Autumn	*Winter*
asters	mahonia
Michaelmas daisy	aconite
sedum autumn joy	heathers
blue flowered salvias	ling
	hellebores
	winter flowering honeysuckle

The History of Gardening

The Old Herbals

For thousands of years herbals were the modern pharmacopeia and the medical textbooks of their day and plants were the medicines prescribed by doctors and surgeons. In 77 AD Dioscorides, the Greek army Doctor who practiced under Nero, wrote *De Materia Medica*, a comprehensive treatise on medicinal plants. He travelled widely and collected plants from all over Southern Europe and North Africa, noting their local names and recording their synonyms. It was an impressive work and it included all the up-to-the-minute knowledge of his day. The trouble was he was so revered that nobody questioned his authority for an astounding 1,500 years.

He and his contemporary, Pliny the Elder—he who recorded the eruption of Vesuvius, but perished in the aftermath—were celebrated as scientific authorities and their work was copied into Latin and Arabic with additions in Turkish and Hebrew, and later translated into French and finally English.

As time went on the true identity of the plants described within the pages of the herbals grew more and more obscure. Copies were made of copies and as nations fought and cities fell libraries were carted off to new lands and were then translated again, often less than accurately. At each copy some detail of the illustrations were lost. Nobody thought to go back to the beginning and make their studies from real plants.

It wasn't until 1492 when Italian university professor Niccolò Leoniceno, studied the newly available Greek edition of Pliny's *Natural History* that the fog began to clear. It was full of anomalies and at last people began to ask questions about the reliability of the old masters.

During the following century, assisted by the invention of the printing press, there was a proliferation of new herbals published in Europe and these began to include plants from much further afield as the world opened up in the Age of Exploration. The need to accurately identify plants took on a new importance.

In 1530 German doctor, Otto Brunsfel published a herbal that was at long last illustrated from real life. But while the text was original and not simply a reworking of the old masters, it was still firmly grounded in folklore and superstition, as indeed were the famous English herbals by John Gerard and John Parkinson that would not be published for another 100 years. Science still lagged behind.

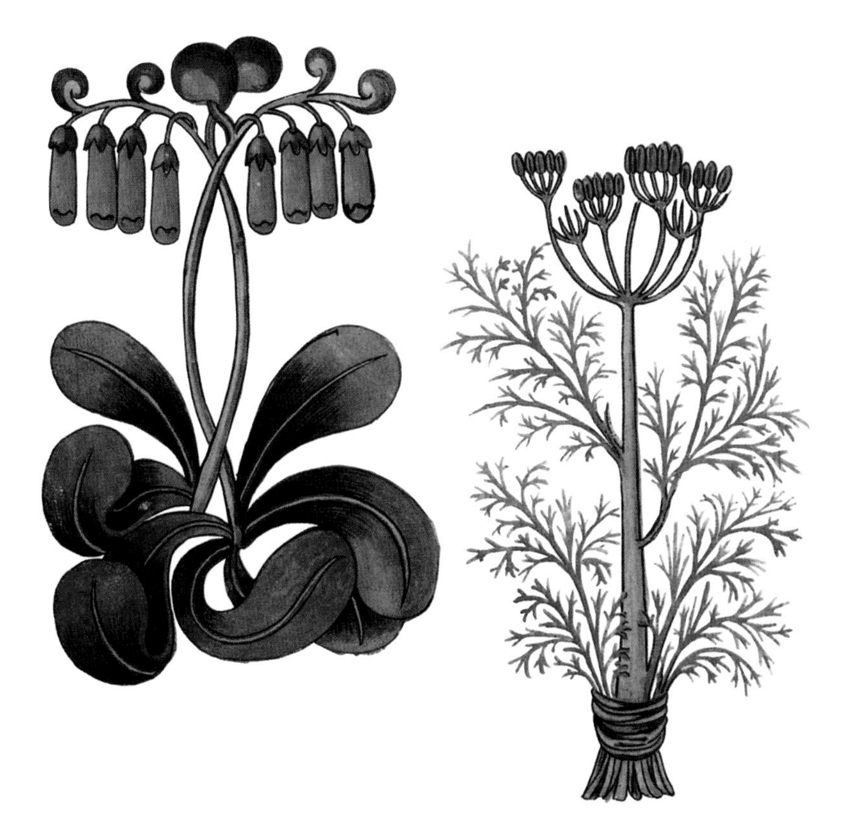

Herbariums

The old herbals, wreathed as they were in mystery, religious prejudice and superstition, did not advance the world of botany or taxonomy one little bit.

Herbariums were the first real step towards the classification of plants. While it seems obvious to us, no one had thought of using real plants to help solve the problem of plant identification. The first herbarium was assembled by the Italian plantsman, lecturer and curator of the first European botanic garden Luca Ghini, while he taught at Pisa University in the 1550s. Ghini mounted dried and pressed specimens collected from the fields and gardens around him, but also used his contacts around Europe to assemble a wider collection of exotic plants. Ghini used his herbarium as a teaching aid and he pioneered a method of recording plants that is practiced by all the botanic gardens of the world to this day. Sadly, his own herbarium is lost. However, his renowned pupil, and successor as director of the garden at Pisa, Andrea Cesalpino assembled his own herbarium which survives to this day, tucked up in the Museum of Natural History in Florence.

Cesalpino was also the first person to classify plants according to their botanical structures, rather than in alphabetical order, or according to their uses. In his seminal work *De plantis libri XVI*, 1583, Cesalpino followed Theophrastus (and Aristotle before him) in wanting a system which was based on the physical similarities and differences of plants and he chose the fruits and seeds of his plants as their defining features. He was closer to a true system of classification than anyone had been before him. It was a leap that seems incredible considering the complete disinterest in progress since the Classical Greek and Roman periods. Alongside his new method of arranging plants he introduced a system of differentiating between very similar plants when he began to offer them up with names that were descriptive.

With the invention of the microscope in 1590 the study of plants and their structures took a great leap forward. A new era of plant science began.

In Europe books were written in Latin, the language of science and scholarship, until well into the seventeenth century and it wasn't uncommon for men of learning to adopt a Latinised version of their names as a badge of refinement.

APIACEAE
Daucus carota L.
Queen Anne's Lace
August 1988

Linnaeus

Over the next 200 years many methods of classification based on the physical characteristics of plants came and went. The descriptive binomial, "two name", system loosely introduced by Cesalpino developed into the unwieldy practice of describing every element of a plant. The tomato, when it first appeared on the scene was called the *Poma DiMori*, "Moors apple", the *Poma d'ori*, "golden apple" or the *Poma amoris*, "the love apple" but was then changed to *Solanum caule inermi herbaceo, foliis pinnatis incisis*, "the solanum with the smooth stem which is herbaceous and has incised pinnate leaves". Thankfully it is now called *Solanum lycopersicum*, the name bestowed on it by Swedish botanist Carolus Linnaeus.

It was Linnaeus (aka Carl Von Linne) who realised that names didn't have to describe plants, they just had to label them and it wasn't until he published his *Species plantarum* in 1753 that a truly universal binomial system was accepted (though it wasn't accepted without a fight from some corners) and with this system came the method by which plants should be sorted. Linnaeus chosle the number and arrangement of stamens and pistils as the defining factors in a highly controversial method that he called the sexual system of classification.

His way of referring to petals as the 'marriage bed', the pistils as 'wives' and 'concubines' and the stamens as 'husbands' along with a few more rather suggestive embellishments lead to him being accused of "loathsome harlotry" and his work condemned as indecent! But despite his wicked ways the system caught on and Linnaeus built himself an empire. He enjoyed a certain amount of power among his peers as men jostled to have plants named after them, and he wasn't opposed to taking advantage of this and was known to name plants of an unpleasant nature or habitat after people he disliked. Famously his opponent Johann Siegesbeck won himself the dubious honour of having a creeping, mud-loving herb, the Siegesbeckia named after him.

Since Linnaeus the system for classification has been refined and changed several times, but his binomial system has remained intact. He was the first to attribute each plant with a family history, so to speak, containing three kingdoms, which were further divided into class, and they, in turn, into order, family, genus, and species. Although we have now discarded his system of classification in favour of looking at the whole plant and studying their genetics and evolution, our system of naming plants still belongs entirely to Linnaeus.

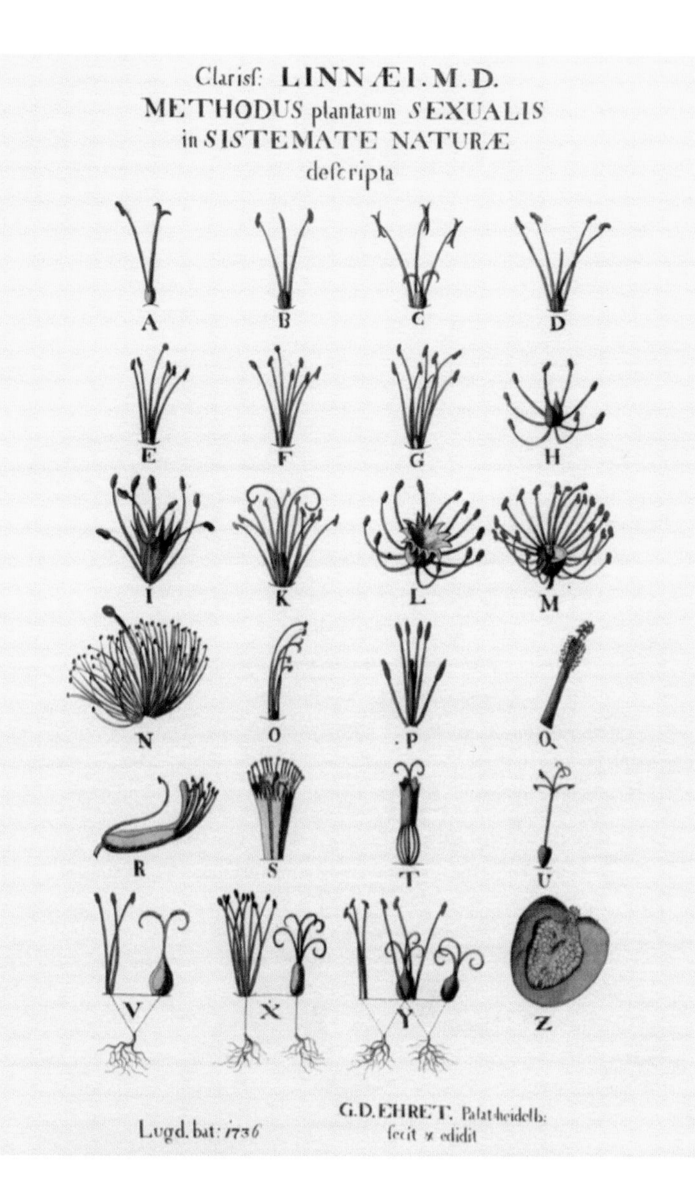
Clarisf: LINNÆI. M. D.
METHODUS plantarum SEXUALIS
in SISTEMATE NATURÆ
descripta
A
B
C
D
E
F
G
H
I
K
L
M
N
O
P
Q
R
S
T
U
V
X
Y
Z
Lugd. bat: 1736
G.D.EHRET. Palat-heidelb:
fecit & edidit

Plant Names

Plant names often cause a great deal of unnecessary anxiety among gardeners. Without a universally recognised system plant catalogues and labels would be meaningless and scientists would be unable to communicate. Latin was the language of scholars when the system was devised so the system is very, very loosely based on Latin.

Official or 'Latin' names can originate from any source. Many of the early taxonomists enjoyed a classical education so there are an abundance of plants named after Greek or Roman myths or gods, such as the genera *Daphne*, *Artemesia* and *Adonis*. They can honour the person who first discovered them, as in the genus *Davidii* which includes the handkerchief tree first discovered by French missionary Père David, or they can be descriptive. Humour is quite often a factor. The botanical name of the giant corpse flower, *Amorphophallus titanium*, translates into "enormous strangely-shaped penis". The various other species belonging to this genus *A pendulus*, *A maximus* and *A impressus* simply add to the ribaldry. A newly discovered fungus from Borneo has been named *Spongiforma squarepantsii* because of its remarkable likeness to a yellow sea sponge, while a blackish-red orchid with outspread petals revels in the name *Dracula vampira*. Occasionally the frustration of distinguishing between numerous similar species is communicated, as in the daisy *Damnxanthodium*.

The only names gardeners need to know are the genus, species and variety (or cultivar). A genus is a group of plants that share a number of permanent characteristics largely confined to that group and can loosely be equated with our surnames. A species is a sub group in a genus, and can be loosely equated to our first names. Varieties are naturally occurring mutations of a species that breed true from seed. A cultivar—short for cultivated variety—is a mutation which occurs as a result of a deliberate cross, like Fairchild's mule or F1 hybrids, or from vegetative propagation, like taking cuttings.

An 'x' appearing before a genus name denotes that this is a plant that resulted from a cross between two genera. An 'x' appearing between the genus and species denotes a cross between two species.

Alatus	winged
Aureus	yellow
Azureus	blue
Barbatus	bearded
Caeruleus	blue
Candidus	shining white
Clavatus	club shaped
Coccineus	scarlet
Conglomeratus	clustered
Contortus	twisted
Cordatus	heart-shaped
Coronarieus	crowned
Crispus	wavy, curled
Decurvus	curved down
Demursus	living under water
Digitalis	fingered
Diffuses	spreading
Ebenus	ebony black
Esculentus	edible
Excelsus	very tall
Extensus	wide
Fasciatus	bound together
Filiformus	thread-like
Floribundus	free-flowering
Frondosus	leafy
Glaber	smooth
Glaucus	grey with waxy bloom
Gracilis	slender
Hirsutus	hairy
Hispidus	bristly
Horridus	very thorny
Humilis	dwarf
Impressus	sunken
Incises	deeply cut
Involutus	rolled inwards
Laciniatus	cut leafed
Latus	broad
Ligulatus	strap like
Lucidus	shining clear
Luteus	yellow
Macranthus	large flowered
Millefolium	thousand leaved
Mollis	soft
Muralis	growing on walls
Nanus	dwarf
Nutans	nodding
Officinalis	medicinal
Orbicularis	disk-shaped
Pallidus	pale
Palustris	of marshy ground
Parvus	small
Pedatu	like a bird's foot
Pinnatus	feathery
Pisiformis	pea shaped
Punctatus	dotted
Radicans	with a distinct root
Reniformis	kidney shaped
Reticulatus	netted
Ruber	red
Rugosus	wrinkled
Sanguineus	blood-red
Sativus	cultivated
Saxitilus	growing on rocks
Scoparius	broom-like
Semperflorens	ever-flowering
Stellatus	star-like
Suffructicosus	shruby
Tardus	late
Tenuis	slender
Tinctus	coloured
Trilobus	three lobed
Uber	luxuriant
Uviformis	like a swarm of bees
Verticillatus	whorled
Villosus	shaggy, hairy
Viridis	green

The international rules of nomenclature now allow plants to be registered under several cultivar or trade names—which rather defeats the point of having one universally recognised name for each plant. It is, like so much else, all about marketing. So beware... that new plant in the nursery catalogue may not be so new after all!

A Brief History of Plant Science & the Plant Hunters

3,500 years ago artists in Nimrod, Mesopotamia carved an image into a stone tablet depicting spiritual beings holding the male flowers of the date palm over the female tree, proving that artificial pollination has been around for a while. Around the same time Egyptian Pharaoh Hatshepsut sent a trading party to the land of Punt, in what is probably present day Somalia, which brought back, among other treasures, 31 live myrrh trees potted up in baskets.

This wasn't an isolated foray; since the beginning of civilisation rulers have understood the power inherent in plants. The Romans were preoccupied with plants for medicine and agriculture and attached great symbolic and religious meaning to many of the 1,500 or so plants that they recognised. Alexander the Great employed naturalists and plant hunters to gather seeds and plants on his campaigns around Egypt, the Middle East and India, and sent them back to the Lyceum in Athens—the school founded by his former tutor, Aristotle and now run by another former pupil of Aristotle, a free-thinker by the name of Theophrastus.

On the occasion of Aristotle's death in 322 BC Theophrastus inherited the stewardship of the Lyceum and together with the works of his former teacher, samples gathered by his own students and the specimens sent to him by Alexander—Theophrastus compiled two scientific treatises on plants that still survive to this day, but only by tremendous good fortune.

Theophrastus was way ahead of his time. He discarded many of the fables and notions of the day in favour of scientific observation. He classified plants under the title of trees, shrubs, undershrubs and herbs instead of by their uses as medicines. He studied life cycles and the effects of geography, soil and climate on growth. He described monocots and dicots, and plant anatomy and physiology, including detailed examinations of flower structures.

After his death, his writings, together with those of Aristotle, were lost to the West for many years. They were passed on, sold, stolen, copied and discarded and only by luck were copies translated into Arabic and held reasonably safe in the libraries of the Middle East. Arab scholars studied those writings and married them with their own investigations into the classification of plants, undertaking experiments and investigations into plant physiology and medicine, as they did in India and further east into China. But while the East revelled in this era of enlightenment, the West sunk into a period of Darkness that would last for another 18 centuries. The progress made by Theophrastus and Aristotle were forgotten. The treatise of Dioscorides (the Greek army doctor) reigned supreme and science stood still.

It wasn't until Theophrastus' *Enquiry into Plants*, which was found languishing on the shelves of the Vatican library in 1483 that the light began to seep in and a new age dawned.

At last in the 1500s the science of botany took off. The invention of the printing press and the microscope and the introduction of anatomically accurate drawings to illustrate the new herbals made the distribution of knowledge and ideas much easier. These, coupled with the descriptive names introduced by Andrea Cesalpino at the University of Pisa suddenly made the world of plants easier to follow. Otto Brunsfels introduced new plants into his beautifully illustrated herbal, rather than simply copying from others. Leonard Fuchs (after whom the Fuchsia is named) lead his students on field trips in search of plants. Until this time it was only the rhizomateuse, the root diggers, who had dirtied their hands. Valerius Cordus recorded in detail the botanical anatomy of flowers for his herbal and travelled widely in search of new medicinal plants. Carolos Clusius (aka Charles de L'Ecluse) plant hunted around Europe, and eventually settled at the University of Leiden, along with his vast collection of plants.

Monasteries had always cultivated plants within their walls, and apothecaries had gathered together the tools of their trade in Physic Gardens, but now the thirst for knowledge and new plants encouraged the Universities of Europe to establish their own collections. Pisa was the first in 1544, followed by Padua a year later.

New plants began flooding in from the New World, and the trickle of introductions brought overland from the East became a flood as Portugal and Spain opened up the sea routes around Africa, Indonesia, and into the southern oceans in their search for spices.

John Parkinson, botanist, apothecary and author of the last of the great English herbals, was also one of the first of a group of men who saw in the new era of enquiry into the world of plants. He funded collecting trips to Arab Spain and North Africa and was instrumental in introducing several new species into England, including the large double Spanish daffodil, as well as cataloguing for the first time some of the native plants of Britain. Parkinson maintained correspondence with people of such diverse botanical interests as the incorrigible plagiarist John Gerard, the adventurous John Tradescant and French plantsmen Matthius de L'Obel (aka Lobelius) and Vespasian Robin, gardener to the King of France.

John Transdescant, Keeper of His Majesty's Gardens, Vines and Silkworms, was one of the first plantsmen whose explorations—modest as they were in light of what was to follow—were documented in detail. He visited the nurseries and gardens of the Low Countries in search of plants to embellish the gardens of his employers, but followed up these modest forays with a trip to Russia, from where he introduced the Cinnamon Rose, *Rosa majalis*, and black, white and red currants, among many other plants. He followed this with collecting trips to the Mediterranean, hitching a ride on a mercenary ship bound to quell the Corsair Pirates, and another on the violent and ill-fated campaign to the Isle de Re. In the late 1630s, a mere 30 years after the establishment of the first colony at Jamestown, Virginia, his son John Tradescant the Younger headed west to search for plants in the New World.

During this time the pace of botanical discovery moved on. Robert Hooke—the first to coin the term 'cell' because the objects he observed through the lens of his microscope reminded him of a monk's cell—published his *Micrographia* in 1665, an exquisitely illustrated book of his microscopic observations of plants and animals. Nehemiah Grew extracted chlorophyll from leaves and concluded that ovules turned into seeds and that pollen was the spermatic fluid produced by the stamens, and in 1716 gardener Thomas Fairchild risked damnation by conducting the first deliberate cross pollination of one species of plant with the other. When, finally, the report of his experiment was presented to the Royal Society Fairchild passed it off as an accidental cross for fear that he would be accused of meddling with creation. Upon his death Fairchild left a legacy of £25 for an annual sermon to be said in praise of the glory of God and his creation.

In 1735 Linnaeus travelled to England in an attempt to gain approval and recognition for his system of classification from the Royal Society and from the great gardeners of the day. Chief of these was Philip Miller.

Miller was the head gardener at the Chelsea Physic Garden for just short of 50 years and the author of the *Gardeners Dictionary*, a universally acclaimed reference which detailed the cultivation of every plant then cultivated in Britain as well as instructions on how to conduct the everyday tasks of gardening and propagation. Miller's gardens would not have been nearly so impressive and his reputation so grand had he not belonged to the growing network of gardeners who exchanged plants, seeds and knowledge. Miller received many of his plants from abroad, and one of his primary sources of material was through the cloth merchant Peter Collinson, and his contact in the colony of America, John Bartram.

John Bartram was the first American plant hunter. He made numerous excursions deep into the country around his home, down into the wilds of Florida and up to the Great Lakes to gather seeds and plants, both to grow in his own garden and to send to his contacts in England. John Bartram's boxes, as they were known, were prized by the merchants and nobility of England, constantly hungry for the fantastic new plants from the young America. The traffic of seeds and plants crossed the ocean in both directions, serving to swell the gardens of Thomas Jefferson's Monticello, George Washington's Mount Vernon and the growing company of American gardeners.

Meanwhile science kept apace and the exploration into the world of plants flourished. Joseph Priestly discovered that the addition of a sprig of mint could reinvigorate the air in a sealed chamber that had been exhausted by the breathing of a mouse, which in turn lead to the discovery by Jan Ingenhousz that this process could only work in the presence of sunlight. They were well on the way to discovering photosynthesis.

In 1768 Captain James Cook set sail on his voyage to record the transit of Venus accompanied by botanists Daniel Solander, former pupil of Carlos Linnaeus, and the wealthy young botanist-explorer, Joseph Banks. Their eventful three year expedition is most celebrated for charting the east coast of Australia, and most notably, Botany Bay, so named because of the vast number of plant specimens that they collected there. On Banks' return he maintained his correspondence with botanists and collectors from all around Europe and the New World and encouraged a network of scientific enquiry and plant hunting that still exists. Banks became the Director of Kew Gardens and the President of the Royal Society and sponsored numerous collecting trips all around the world in search of new plants.

In 1772 Scottish gardener Francis Masson was the first collector to be sent out of Kew on a plant hunting expedition when he sailed with Captain Cook to South Africa. His journey was fantastic in the light of the times; the land was unexplored and incredibly dangerous and he endured attacks by insects, animals and escaped convicts on his expeditions across the tropical wilderness. But his journey was a success and Masson was responsible for introducing over half the known population of pelargonium species to Britain as well as the Bird of Paradise *Strelitzia reginae* and the Arum Lily, *Zantedeschia aethiopica* among many others. Masson continued plant hunting for 33 years in the Canaries, the Azores and the West Indies. His last voyage was to Canada where he died, aged 54.

Masson's lead was followed by a proliferation of plant hunters who ventured into the new territories under the direction of Joseph Banks and his successors at Kew Gardens and the Royal Horticultural Society.

Five years after the death of the illustrious Banks the new director at Kew, William Hooker, sent another young botanist-gardener to America. David Douglas, a natural adventurer, is most noted for his introduction of many conifers including the Noble Fir, *Abies nobilis* as well as shrubs such as *Mahonia aquifolium* and the garden staple, *Ribes sanguineum*. In all, his wild adventures resulted in 200 new species of plants being introduced into Britain. After a thrilling career as a collector Douglas, aged just 35, died in suspicious circumstances while collecting in Hawaii.

One of the most celebrated plant hunters of his age was the tea thief, Robert Fortune who secured his place in history by transporting 20,000 illegally procured tea plants from China to India. In the hostile political climate Fortune often disguised himself as a local merchant by shaving his head, and dressing in peasant clothes. Fortune introduced 120 plants to Western gardens including the bleeding heart, *Dicentra spectablis* and the ubiquitous *Weigela rosea.*

Meanwhile, back in Britain in 1831 botany lecturer John Stevens Henslow recommended his pupil Charles Darwin accompany Captain Fitzroy on the voyage of the Beagle. In the same year Henslow oversaw the transformation of the old physic garden at Cambridge into the new Botanical Garden, the first University garden in England, This new garden, stocked by the great plant hunters of the time, displayed Henslow's interest and investigation into the classification of plants, the placement of plants in species groups and the incidents of natural mutations and variations.

A few years later Gregor Mendel conducted his genetic experiments on peas, Robert Brown detected the nucleus of a cell and Charles Darwin and Alfred Russell Wallace presented their theory of evolution to the Royal Society.

Spain and Portugal continued to receive new plant introductions from their colonies in South America and collectors sent from Scotland, Vienna and from La Jardin du Roi in Paris, along with many French missionary botanists, added to the ranks of new plants. One of the least known but most prolific expeditions of its time was the United States Exploring Expedition in 1838–1842 which brought back 50,000 dried botanical specimens of 10,000 species along with 1,000 living plants and 648 species of seeds from all over the world. These along with the other natural history specimens and artefacts collected on the voyage formed the foundation of the collections at the new Smithsonian Institute.

Joseph Hooker, son of William, was also a fine plant hunter with a taste for adventure. His first expedition was with Captain James Clark Ross to pinpoint the position of the magnetic South Pole, stopping *en route* to collect specimens on three continents. Several years later Hook headed east for an action-packed expedition to hunt for Rhododendrons in the Himalayas and in 1871, together with the foremost American botanist, Asa Gray he journeyed across the towering mountains of the western United States in order to compare the flora with that of eastern Asia and Japan before returning to England with 1,000 dried specimens to swell the herbarium at Kew.

In 1899, Earnest Henry Wilson, just 23 years old, set off for China with instructions to find a tree. The tree, known from accounts by French missionary, Pere David, was the beautiful and elusive *Davidii involucrata*, the handkerchief tree. At last he tracked down the single specimen, but all that was left was a stump standing beside a newly built wooden hut. He had travelled 13,000 miles for nothing. Resolute, he set off again to continue his search and after a further 24 days of trekking through remote and dangerous country he finally stumbled on a magnificent specimen. His collection swelled with seeds and cuttings from the *Davidii* and thousands of other trees, shrubs and herbaceous plants, he turned for home. Wilson's plant hunting career continued for a further 28 years and in that time he introduced a vast number of stunning plants to the west including such garden gems as the regal lily, *Lillium regale*, *Clematis armandii*, *Cornus kousa chinensis*, *Viburnum davidii*, *Acer griseum*, and *Kolkwitzia amabilis*.

Many more intrepid plant hunters have travelled the world in search of new plants to adorn the gardens of the world and the stories of their expeditions and the plants they brought back are fascinating. Today plant hunters and botanists continue to search out new plants and make amazing discoveries. They still collect dried specimens to add to the herbariums of the great botanic gardens of the world, and they gather seeds and live plants from forests and jungles, just as the old plant hunters used to do, but today they are using the information to piece together the history of plant life on Earth, and to find and preserve whole species before they disappear forever.

There is still a lot to do.

Timeline of Garden History: Selected Dates Through the Ages

3000 BC — Written guides for the use of medicinal plants are available in Mesopotamia and China. Potatoes are grown in Peru. Egyptians are making and wearing cotton clothes. Tomb paintings show walled gardens with fish ponds and fruit trees. Farming thrives in India.

1550 BC — Queen Hatshepsut of Egypt commissions the first recorded plant hunting expedition to gather plants and other riches from the land of Punt.

1495 BC — One of the oldest surviving garden plans is drawn up for the garden of a court official in the Egyptian city of Thebes.

384 BC / *372 BC* — Birth of Aristotle, the great natural philosopher who ran the Peripatetic School at the Lyceum in Athens, and counted Alexander the Great among his pupils. / Alexander the Great employs a plantsman to collect and ship plants back to Artistotle and Theophrastus from his excursions.

336 BC — Birth of Theophrastus. His magnificent treatises on plants and gardening would not be improved upon for a staggering 2,000 years.

200 BC — The Hopewellian farming culture in Eastern North America is thriving.

44 AD — Romans invade Britain.

77 — Pliny publishes his *Natural History*, a work which drew upon many historical and contemporary sources including Theophrastus. He was a great chronicler of the knowledge of the natural world of his time./ Dioscorides, the Greek doctor who practiced under Nero, writes *De materia medica*, which is used as the foremost medical and botanical reference for the next 1,200 years.

670 — St Fiacre, patron saint of gardeners, dies.

1066 — William the Conqueror kills King Harold at the Battle of Hastings.

1191 — China exports tea for the first time.

1225 — Cotton manufacturing established in Spain.

1227 — Vatican botanical garden is founded.

1295 — Marco Polo returns from his epic journey to China along the silk route.

1440 — The invention of the Guttenberg Press facilitates the widespread distribution of maps, books and treatise.

1453 — Turks invade Constantinople, closing down overland trade routes.

1483 — Publication of the translation of *Aristotle and Theophrastus* by Teodoro of Gaza marks the end of the dark ages of plant science.

1492 — Christopher Columbus sets sail from Spain. This marks the beginning of plant exchanges between Europe and the Americas.

1500's — botanical illustrators finally begin working from live specimens, and illustrations in herbals begin to be accurate as well as attractive.

1505 — Leonardo de Vinci begins work on the *Mona Lisa*.

1525 — Richard Banckes publishes the first English herbal.

1530 — Otto Brunfels' herbal, *Herbarum Vivai Eicones* with its lifelike woodcut illustrations marks the beginning of a new era in plant identification.

1544 — Europe's first botanic garden is established in Pisa by botany professor Luca Ghini.

1534 — Jacques Cartier enters the St Lawrence River. Land in Great Lakes is claimed for France.

1555 — Carolus Clusius, Dutch botanist, grows tulip bulbs imported from Constantinople.

1569 — Nicolas Monardes of Spain writes *Joyfull Newes out of the Newe Found Worlde*, a treatise about the plants which had begun to arrive from the Americas.

1570 — Mathias L'Obel (Lobelius) publishes his *Stripium adversaria nova*. The illustrations for this herbal later illustrated works by Dodoens, de L'Ecluse and Gerards famous English herbal.

1583 — Cesalpino classifies plants according to their fruits and flowers in his work, *De Plantis*. His herbarium, the oldest in the world, survives to this day.

1586 — Sir Francis Drake and Walter Raleigh bring sassafras and potatoes to England.

1590 — Zacharias Janssen develops the first compound microscope.

1597 — Gerard's herbal is published, as is Shakespeare's *Romeo and Juliet*.

1601 — Charles De L'Ecluse (Carolus Clusius) travels around Europe and the Near East. He published *Rariorum Plantarum historia* and introduced many bulbs into the Low Countries including ranunculus, anemone, iris, and narcissus.

1618 — John Tradescant the Elder sets off on his first plant hunting expedition to Russia. This was followed by trips to the Canaries and the Mediterranean.

1621 — The first American Thanksgiving feast was celebrated by the pilgrims and Massasoit Indians. / Oxford Botanic Garden, the first in England, is established.

1629 — John Parkinson's *Paradisi in sole paradisus terrestris* is published.

1633 — Galileo is tried and convicted because of his assertions that the earth orbits the sun.

1634 — Tulipomania engulfs Holland.

1637 — John Tradescant the younger travels to Virginia "to gather up all raritye of flowers, plants and shells."

1648 — Jean Baptiste van Helmont performs an experiment proposed by Nicholas of Cusa nearly 200 years earlier in which a willow is weighed, then planted in a weighed amount of soil. After five years, the final weights of plant and soil, as well as the total weight of water applied, are added together and compared to the initial weights. Van Helmont concludes that the increased mass of the plant derived from water rather than soil.

1660 — The Royal Society of London for Improving Natural Knowledge is established to support the pursuit and dissemination of new ideas in science.

1661 — Malpighi observes capillaries in plants. / Louis the XIV asked Andre Le Notre to design the grounds at his Chateau at Versailles.

1665 — Robert Hooke publishes *Micrographia*.

1673 — Founding of the Chelsea Physic Garden by the Society of Apothecaries of London.

1674 — Leeuwenhoek observes and describes bacteria and protozoa with the aid of his microscope.

1682 — John Ray devises a system which classifies plants by overall morphology and divides flowering plants into monocots and dicots.

1701 — The first agricultural machine, the seed drill, is invented by Jethro Tull.

1717 — Thomas Fairchild produces the first man-made plant hybrid by crossing a dianthus and a carnation.

1727 — Stephen Hales writes that plant leaves "very probably" take in nourishment from the air, and that light may also be involved.

1731 — First edition of Philip Miller's *Gardener's dictionary*.

1732 — Philip Miller of the Chelsea Physic Garden sends the first cotton seeds to Georgia, USA.

1733 — John Bartram, American farmer, began sending seed boxes from Philadelphia to London merchant, Peter Collinson, a passionate plant collector.

1735 — Carolus Linnaeus writes *System Naturae* to classify all living things.

1753 — Roses from China begin arriving in Europe. / Linnaeus publishes his *Species Plantarum*, the basis for the system of nomenclature that is still used today.

1759 — Kew gardens are created. In 1840 the gardens are adopted as the National Botanic Garden. / George Washington settles at Mount Vernon and begins to lay out the gardens as they can be seen today.

1766 — Joseph Banks goes plant collecting in Newfoundland and Labrador.

1768 — James Cook begins the first of his Pacific explorations accompanied by Joseph Banks and Danial Solander.

1770 — Thomas Jefferson moved to Monticello, near Charlottesville, Virginia, and soon after begins work on the gardens which would occupy him for the rest of his life. / Cook discovers Australia.

1771 — Joseph Priestley discovers that air which has been exhausted by the breathing of animals or burning of a candle can be restored by the introduction of a green plant. He isolates the gas later identified as oxygen.

1772 — Francis Masson, the first official plant hunter sent out of Kew, accompanies Captain Cook on his second circumnavigation of the globe. Masson introduces the bird of paradise, *Strelitzia reginae*, and the white arum lily, *Zantedeschia aethiopica* among many others.

1775 — The American War of Independence begins.

1779 — Jan Ingenhousz discovers that only the green parts of plants release oxygen and only when they are in sunlight.

1804 — Nicolas de Saussure establishes the basic equation of photosynthesis: a process in which a green plant illuminated by sunlight takes in carbon dioxide and water and converts them into organic material and oxygen.

1804 Thomas Andrew Knight becomes president of the Horticultural Society of London, later named the Royal Horticultural Society, a position he held until his death in 1838. Knight conducted numerous experiments on plant breeding, using peas as his subjects, and distinguished between gymnosperms and angiosperms.

1819 Patrick Shirreff begins a series of experiments on the hybridisation of wheat.

1825 David Douglas, plant collector, is sent to North America by the RHS.

1829 Nathanial Bagshaw Ward designs the Wardian Case which allowed the transportation of thousands of plants around the globe.

1830 The lawn mower is invented in England by Edwin Beard Budding.

1831 Darwin sets sail on *The Beagle*. / Robert Brown identifies the nucleus of a cell. Brown is also known for accompanying Mathew Flinders on his exploration of Australia. He later became the Keeper of the botanical Department of the British Museum.

1837 René Dutrochet makes the connection between chlorophyll and the ability of plants to assimilate carbon dioxide.

1841 Irish potato famine begins.

1845 Julius Robert von Mayer suggests that the sun is the ultimate source of energy used by living organisms, and that photosynthesis is a conversion of light energy into chemical energy.

1851 Sir Joseph Paxton's giant greenhouse, the Crystal Palace, is erected in Hyde Park.

1858 Darwin and Wallace report their Theory of Evolution to the Royal Society. / Frederick Law Olmsted and Calvert Vaux win a competition to design Central Park in New York.

1859 The bedding plant system is very popular. 40,000 bedding plants are planted in Hyde Park, London.

1866 The monk, Gregor Mendel, presents his findings on the breeding of peas to his local horticultural society… nobody pays much attention.

1871 Plant explorer Marianna North sets off to observe plants in Canada, Japan, Brazil, Java and Ceylon.

1877 Asa Grey and Joseph Dalton Hooker travel to the Western USA to catalogue new plant species.

1893 Gertrude Jekyll takes up gardening and introduces a new style of informal planting.

1894 — Iceberg lettuce is introduced by W Atlee Burpee & Co.

1899 — Ernest 'Chinese' Wilson set off on the first of his adventures into China in search of new plants. Among his most famous introductions was the handkerchief tree, *Davidii involucrata*.

1900 — Mendel's work is rediscovered.

1905 — Blackman shows that photosynthesis involves both "light" and "dark" reactions.

1932 — Kroll and Ruska invent the first electron microscope.

1935 — Fritz Zernicke invents the first phase contrast microscope.

1953 — Francis Crick and James Watson provide a model for DNA.

1956 — Melvin Calvin uses radioactively labeled $14CO^2$ to reveal the pathway of carbon assimilation in photosynthesis. Calvin is awarded Nobel Prize in 1961.

1960 — Robert Woodward synthesizes chlorophyll. Awarded Nobel Prize, 1965.

1962 — Rachel Carson's *Silent Spring* is published.

1972 — DDT is banned in US.

1994 — The Flavr Savr tomato is the first genetically modified food to go on sale to the public.

Black Dog Publishing Limited
10A Acton Street
London
WC1X 9NG

t. +44 (0)207 713 5097
f. +44 (0)207 713 8682
e. info@blackdogonline.com

Designed at Black Dog Publishing
with thanks to Aurora Moreno Pavón

British Library Cataloguing-in-Publication Data.
A CIP record for this book is available from the
British Library.

ISBN 978 1 907317 71 2

Black Dog Publishing is an environmentally responsible company. *A Pocket Guide to Plants and Gardening* is printed on FSC accredited paper.

Also available:
Kids in the Wild Garden
Kids in the Garden: Growing Plants for Food and Fun
Growing Stuff: An Alternative Guide to Gardening

architecture art design
fashion history photography
theory and things

www.blackdogonline.com